THEIR BLOOD STILL CRIES OUT

CLEANSING LIVES AND LAND FROM THE CONSEQUENCES OF ANTI-SEMITISM

KEN HEPWORTH

Zaccmedia

Published by Zaccmedia
www.zaccmedia.com
info@zaccmedia.com

Published November 2013

Copyright © 2013 Ken Hepworth

The right of Ken Hepworth to be identified as author of
this work has been asserted by him in accordance with the
Copyright, Designs and Patents Act 1988.

British Library Cataloguing-in-Publication Data
A catalogue record for this book is available from
the British Library

ISBN: 978-1-909824-03-4

CONTENTS

PREFACE   1

INTRODUCTION   5

CHAPTER 1   GOD'S PRESENT AND FUTURE   11
RELATIONSHIP TO ISRAEL AND ITS LAND

CHAPTER 2   THE SIGNIFICANCE OF ISRAEL AND   35
CHRISTIAN ANTI-SEMITISM

CHAPTER 3   THE CURSE OF ANTI-SEMITISM   73
AND ITS CONSEQUENCES

CHAPTER 4   HOW TO CLEANSE THE LAND   109
FROM BLOODGUILT

CHAPTER 5   AUTHORITY AND POWER IN   137
INTERCESSORY PRAYER

ABOUT THE AUTHOR   159

PREFACE

It has not been an easy task to write this book. It is written out of a love for Jewish people and compassion for their long history of suffering through persecution. In 1993, Yitzhak Rabin said: 'We have come from an anguished and grieving land ... from a people ... that has not known a single year – not a single month – in which mothers have not grieved for their sons.'[1] The day is coming when the living God will be glorified amongst the nations for all He has promised to do for Israel (Ezekiel 36:23). I have also written from a genuine concern for the body of Christ that is largely unaware of God's continuing relationship with Israel, and seems oblivious to events that are to occur before the return of Messiah Jesus, some of which are happening before our very eyes (Jeremiah 31:10). Referring to Jesus, Acts 3:19 says: '... whom heaven must receive until the times of restoration of all things, which God has spoken by the mouth of all His holy prophets since the world began.'

A plain reading of the Bible makes it clear Israel as a nation is a vital part of the restoration of all things. The prophets prophesied a time when Israel's exile would end and there would be a physical and spiritual restoration of Israel (Jeremiah 16:14,15). However, the Church is deeply affected by the spiritualising of prophecy and by anti-Semitism, and cannot see this. I intend to highlight the presence of ant-Semitism in various places including the Church. This will serve two purposes. One is to reveal from the Bible God's view of anti-Semitism. The other is to provide biblical principles for cleansing land and lives from the severe consequences of anti-Semitism.

One of the challenges in writing anything on Israel and the Middle East is that events happen so quickly. As someone has said, 'we live in the days of sudden'. There is no doubt that Israel is facing the most dangerous existential threat since the birth of the nation some 3,500 years ago. Iran is very close to having a nuclear option. There is much debate about whether or not Iran would use such a weapon against Israel. If words mean anything, then Iran's threat to wipe out Israel is no empty threat.[2] The world may continue to hope for a diplomatic solution. Israel, however, cannot afford to base the security of its people on such a chance. Jews in the Diaspora made such a mistake in the 1930s with the speeches of Adolf Hitler; when they could have escaped Europe, the majority of Jews stayed were they were, and consequently became victims of one of the darkest and most evil times in the whole of Jewish and world history.

In 2009, I was privileged along with two Ebenezer team members to accompany an *aliyah* flight to Israel. On board was a wonderful lady called Lena. She was 92 years old and was the last member of her family to make *aliyah*. Not only so, but Lena, along with her mother, was one of the last Jewish people to flee Austria before the doors closed and no Jewish person was allowed to leave. Those who remained were consumed in the crematoria of the Nazi death camps. What prompted the decision to leave? It was the arrest and brutal treatment of her Jewish employer. He was forcefully taken away from his shoe factory, and never seen again. It was this incident that led Lena and her mother to decide their home in Austria, where they had been born and educated, was no longer a safe place.

I am grateful to my wife, Jean, for faithfully encouraging me to persevere in researching and writing. My thanks go to Lissa Smith for the very helpful suggestions she offered, as well as her patience and tenacity in the editing process of this book. I am also grateful to Paul Stanier of Zaccmedia for his help in publishing this book.

Ken Hepworth
Autumn 2013

INTRODUCTION

The forerunner to this book, *Reclaiming the Ground*[3] focused on the theme of land and buildings and how they can be defiled though human sin, which gives access to unclean spirits. In the following chapters we will consider a particular land, Israel, and a particular people, the Jews. Dealing with curses will continue to be the subject here, but this time we shall be looking at curses sent by the living God upon those who seek to harm His covenant nation, Israel, and His chosen people, the Jews. We shall focus on the consequences of anti-Semitism. Of particular concern in this context is how land and lives can be cleansed from the curses that follow the shedding of Jewish blood.

For some believers the mention of the word 'Israel' produces either a negative reaction or, perhaps even worse, no reaction at all. Indifference and silence in the face of Jewish suffering is by far the most common reaction of many Christians, and sadly has been so throughout history. Silence in the face of evil amounts to a shared guilt. Although there are exceptions, many pastors are all too aware that to teach the future physical and spiritual restoration of Israel in their sermons, will in most cases polarise their congregations. It is my hope that pastors who read this book will begin fearlessly to challenge the false hermeneutic behind Replacement Theology. Many Christians consciously – and some unconsciously – believe that God has finished with the nation of Israel, and that it no longer has any relevance, as the Church is now the 'new Israel'. As if the living God would fail to fulfil all the promises that He made to Abraham! To believe this is a serious error, as I hope to prove from Scripture. It is an indictment against humanity that the word 'Jew' is still used some sixty-eight years after the Holocaust – known to the Jewish people as the HaShoah, meaning desolation – as a curse word. In order to fully appreciate the evil of anti-Semitism, and more importantly, how God views it, it is necessary to have some understanding of the significance of Israel to the living God. It is often overlooked that God has forever linked His holy name with the fathers of the nation of Israel – Abraham, Isaac and Jacob (Exodus 3:6).

> Moreover God said to Moses, 'Thus you shall say to the children of Israel: 'The LORD God of your fathers, the God of Abraham, the God of Isaac, and the God of Jacob, has sent me to you. This is My name forever, and this is My memorial to all generations.
>
> (EXODUS 3:15)

The New Testament continues to refer to God in the same way (Matthew 22:32). To this very day, and throughout eternity, God remains the same; He will forever be the God of Abraham, Isaac and Jacob.[4] In fact, the names of the twelve tribes of Israel are written on the twelve gates in the heavenly Jerusalem (Revelation 21:12). Therefore, in the first two chapters we will look at the choice of Israel by God, His relationship with the nation of Israel, and the significance of Israel to God's plan for the salvation of humankind and the future reign upon earth of His Son, Yeshua Ha-Mashiach – Jesus, the Messiah. The early chapters will also include a brief look at Israel in world opinion and the relationship between Israel and the Palestinian Arab/Muslim world, including their claim to the land of Israel with east Jerusalem as the capital of a future Palestinian state.

Whilst this book is written mainly for the benefit of those who are called to pray for and to intercede for Israel, it is my hope that it will also benefit those who have not yet received God's revelation concerning the nation of Israel, and are unaware of end-time prophecy regarding the physical and spiritual restoration of Israel (Ezekiel 36,37). For those who would like to read more on the significance of the nation, many good books are available that deal with the place of Israel in the will and purposes of God as recorded in the Bible, written by authors such as Lance Lambert, Derek Prince, Murray Dixon, Ken Burnett, Reverend Willem Glashouwer, and many others. A good book to begin with is by Steve Malz.[5] This present book is written to expose the consequences of anti-Semitism, and to provide biblical principles for cleansing land and lives that have been cursed through the shedding of Jewish blood.

There is only one Saviour for the whole of humankind. 'Nor is their salvation in any other, for there is no other name under heaven given among men by which we must be saved' (Acts 4:12; see John 14:6). I do not believe that there is a separate way of salvation for Jew and Gentile. At this present time Israel as a nation does not recognise that Jesus Christ – Yeshua Ha-Maschiach – is their Saviour sent by the living God in fulfilment of biblical prophecy. The apostle Paul makes it clear in Romans chapters 9, 10 and 11 that God has not cast away His people, but He has given them a spirit of stupor and eyes that cannot see until the fullness of the Gentiles has come in, after which the deliverer will come out of Zion and, so all Israel will be saved (Romans 11: 25–27). If God were to cast Israel aside because of their sin, then Christians have no real assurance of salvation. Idolatry and immorality, the sins for which Israel stands condemned, have been and are currently present in the Church. God is a covenant-keeping God. Both Jew and Gentile stand together at the foot of the cross in need of forgiveness (Romans 1–3). According to the prophet Zechariah, the day will come when their eyes of the nation of Israel will be opened, and the God of Abraham, Isaac and Jacob, the Father of our Lord Jesus, will pour out upon them the spirit of grace and supplication (Zechariah 12:10–14).

I believe that our chief responsibility as Gentile believers towards our Jewish brethren is to testify by our lives and our love for them that Jesus is Israel's Messiah. We are to provoke them to jealousy (Romans 11:11,14). We can only do this by loving them unconditionally and by praying for them. One of the issues that Christians must recognise, if they are to be effective in commending their Saviour, are the many years of Christian persecution that come between Jew and Christian. Most Christians are unaware of how Jews have been treated by the established Church through the ages. For a history of Christian persecution of Jews, may I recommend: *The Anguish of the Jews: Twenty-three Centuries of Antisemitism* by Edward H. Flannery, a Stimulus Book published in 1985 in the USA. Also, *Father, Forgive Us: A Christian Response to the Chruch's Heritage of Jewish Persecution*, by Fred Wright, Monarch Books, published in 2002.

In this book I have attempted to present historical and biblical facts, concerning which there is widespread ignorance. My aim has been to bring relevant scriptures from the whole Bible in support of the Lord's continuing relationship with the nation of Israel.

I believe that the redemption purchased by the blood of Christ is more than sufficient to atone for the sins of the whole human race, although it is only effective for those who are willing to receive it, and who meet the condition of repentance from sin and faith in the atoning sacrifice of Jesus upon the cross. This includes all those who are ensnared by the many religions of the world. It also includes the Palestinian Arabs, who clearly have no love for Jews, but God loves them no more or less than you or I. However, if Muslims are to be saved from the consequences of sin, they will have to accept a Jewish Messiah.

I believe that the Bible is the Word of God, and not that it merely contains His Word. The last words of King David testify to this: 'The Spirit of the LORD spoke by me, And His word was on my tongue' (2 Samuel 23:2). 'knowing this first, that no prophecy of Scripture is of any private interpretation, for prophecy never came by the will of man, but holy men of God spoke as they were moved by the Holy Spirit' (2 Peter 1:20,21). 'All Scripture is given by inspiration of God'

(2 Timothy 3:16). 'The Greek word translated 'inspiration' is *theopneustos*. It means 'God-breathed' Prophecy did not originate from humanity; God Himself initiated it and the Scripture is the Word of God.

In contrast to the allegorical method of Bible exegesis, I believe that the best way to read the Bible is the literal, grammatical and historical way. Which simply means, when the Bible makes plain sense, seek no other sense.[6] My own understanding is still growing and I am aware that it is not complete. As it says in the study helps of the New King James Version (this Bible version is used throughout the book), '... meaning is singular, not plural ...' The interpretation is what the writer intended with the vocabulary he used.[7] There may be more than one application, but no more than one meaning. The key to understanding God's Word is the Holy Spirit. I am well aware that Christians who hold a similar view of the inspiration of Scripture will take a different position concerning Israel. It was a combination of anti-Semitism and the use of the allegorical method of Bible interpretation that led the early Church fathers to teach that God had rejected the Jews who had now been replaced by the Church, which according to them is the 'new Israel'. Consequently, Replacement Theology is sown into the very fabric of the Church. The Bible is clear that it is possible for each of us as genuine believers to be deceived, (Matthew 24: 44; 2 Corinthians 11:3). I only ask that with God's help the reader allows the Scriptures to speak for themselves. I have attempted, to the best of my ability, to present biblical truth.

Chapter 1

God's Present and Future Relationship to Israel and its Land

... I will bless those who bless you, And I will curse him who curses you; And in you all the families of the earth shall be blessed.

(Genesis 12:3)

God's promise to the Jewish people still stands, and while some individuals and nations have been blessed for blessing the nation of Israel, others have been cursed.

When my enemies turn back, They shall fall and perish at Your presence. For You have maintained my right and my cause; You sat on the throne judging in righteousness. You have rebuked the nations, You have destroyed the wicked; You have blotted out their name forever and ever. O enemy, destructions are finished forever! And you have destroyed cities; Even their memory has perished.

(Psalm 9:3–6)

This book highlights the terrible consequences of anti-Semitism and the shedding of Jewish blood. God never forgets the slaying of the least one of the descendants of Abraham, Isaac and Jacob. To comprehend the gravity of this, we will first consider what the nation of Israel and the Jewish people mean to the Lord, a topic clearly revealed in Scripture. When God's elect people are slaughtered simply because they are Jewish, the Lord takes this very personally, because Israel is His firstborn son, and those who touch Israel touch the apple of His eye (Exodus 4:22; Zechariah 2:8).

Once we see God's heart for Israel, we will gain a much clearer understanding of His character and His purposes. It will lead us to a greater respect for the truth and practical outworking of the Word of God.

As we recognise the effects of the curse levelled on those who curse the Jews, we will also learn the remedy – how to ask the Lord to remove the curse and bring restoration. This can help open the door for *aliyah*, the return of the Jewish people to the land of Israel which God promised them.

> Hear the word of the LORD, O nations, and declare it in the isles afar off, and say, 'He who scattered Israel will gather him, And keep him as a shepherd does his flock.' For the LORD has redeemed Jacob, And ransomed him from the hand of one stronger than he.
>
> (JEREMIAH 31:10,11)

ISRAEL AND WORLD OPINION

Israel is continually in the spotlight in world news. The media would have us believe that Israel is a rogue state. During UN meetings in New York, September 2011, the Palestinian president applied for recognition for the state of Palestine with east Jerusalem as its capital. Direct negotiations with Israel were bypassed, as the Palestinian leadership had already withdrawn from peace negotiations. When the actual vote came on 29 November 2012, some 140 UN nations out of 173 voted in favour of this proposal, and Palestine was granted observer status. The United Nations has passed more resolutions condemning Israel than any other nation.[8] Recently, the secretary general of the United Nations in answering a Jewish student confirmed that the UN is biased against the Israeli people and the Israeli government. He went on to say that it was, 'an unfortunate situation'.[9]

THE NATIONS AND THEIR SOLUTION

The current Palestinian demand to push Israel back to the 1967 Green Line is in reality the 1949 armistice lines, and the place where military action ceased in 1949. Israel regards this Green Line as indefensible. President Obama is also pushing for this solution, and there seems general agreement among the nations on this.[10] This is also the current position of the European Union.[11]

It seems the nations of the world are determined to divide the land of Israel, and to agree to east Jerusalem becoming the capital of a new Palestinian state in which Jews would not be allowed to live or even to have access. This has been clearly stated and means that no Jew would be allowed to pray at the Western Wall, a most sacred Jewish site. It was on the 30 July 1980 that the Knesset –the Jewish parliament – declared that Jerusalem is 'the eternal and undivided capital of the Jewish people'. Since then it appears that there has been a worldwide increase of anti-Semitism. For actual figures, please see annual reports on world-wide anti-Semitism produced by the CST (Community Service Trust),[12] and 'Anti-Semitism Worldwide – 2008/9' (2010, pp. 318), produced by the Stephen Roth Institute for the Study of Contemporary Anti-Semitism and Racism.[13]

THE NEW ANTI-SEMITISM IS THE OLD ONE WEARING NEW CLOTHES

The term anti-Semitism was brought into common use in 1897 by an anti-Jewish German called Wilhelm Marr, as a euphemism for the German word *Judenhass* which literally means hatred of the Jews.[14] There is some evidence that the term may have been used earlier that this. This term is given more detailed explanation in chapter 3.

DELEGITIMISATION

Israel is facing a barrage of hostility via the Internet and from various protest groups that are active in stirring up hatred against Israel. Their main weapons are false accusation based on unsubstantiated facts. According to the delegitimisers, Israel has no right to exist as a nation. In the twenty-first century, anti-Semitism is now being widely expressed through movements that are hostile to Israel, such as the Palestine Solidarity Campaign. This organisation is based in Edinburgh, but has branches throughout the UK and is very active in stirring up action against Israel. To quote from their website: 'Israel continues to build illegal settlements and the wall, controls Gaza, denies Palestinian refugees their right to return, grows produce and sets up industrial zones on stolen Palestinian land. Only international pressure can deliver a just peace for Palestinians.'[15]

In this quote, the phrases 'illegal settlements' and 'stolen 'Palestinian land' are both incorrect. The average reader is likely to swallow this line and judge that Israel is in the wrong. But how many would take the time to check if these statements are true? The PSC also promotes the boycotting of Israeli goods made in the incorrectly named 'occupied territories'; they are more correctly described as disputed territories.

THE BDS CAMPAIGN

According to the BDS website (Boycott, Divestment and Sanctions), the movement attempts to boycott Israeli academics and Israeli cultural events, and those who perform at such events, musicians and actors.[16] Pressure is applied to those who would perform in Israel as well as in the UK. A recent example from the Palestine Solidarity Campaign – part of the BDS Campaign – based in Cardiff concerns the well-known singer Tom Jones. He received a letter from this group, and has been pressured not to perform his forthcoming concert (27 August 2013) in Tel Aviv. To quote from *The Daily Telegraph* article: 'We hope Tom Jones will change his mind once he learns how this gig will be used to normalize Israel's ongoing atrocities against the Palestinian People.'[17] Unless one is aware of the facts, a word such as 'atrocities' could frighten an individual. These 'requests' have been reinforced by email threats from anti-Israel campaigners.

A similar pressure has led to universities withdrawing invitations from visiting Israeli academics lecturing in the United Kingdom (a repeat of the 1930s situation in Nazi Germany). The boycotting is aimed at supermarkets and shops that stock Israeli products made in the disputed territories.

According the BDS website, the aim of divestment is as follows:

> Divestment calls for the withdrawal of stocks and funds from corporations complicit in the violation of international law and Palestinian rights and ensures that investment portfolios and public funds are not used to finance or purchase products and services from such companies. These campaigns can take advantage of voluntary and mandatory corporate responsibility mechanisms.[18]

Sanctions are aimed at Israel's military, economic and even diplomatic links.

> There are three areas to which sanctions can be applied: military links, including partnerships, agreements and joint operations; economic links, including trade, co-operation, forums, agreements, and joint research initiatives; and diplomatic links, including relations on an official level, participation in international institutions, external forums and networks and meetings between state representatives.[19]

Readers must judge for themselves whether this kind of action, fuelled as it is by anti-Semitism, is likely to lead to a peaceful resolution. To treat Israel as a pariah state when it is the only democracy in the Middle East is unjust and unfair. In Israel, women and Arab citizens are treated equally; this is not so in Arab countries. Israel is a sovereign state with a defence force (the IDF) that unlike other nations, such as the

UK and the USA, only engages in defence of its citizens and is accountable to the Knesset. Colonel Richard Kemp, a former British Army commander of British forces in Afghanistan, is on record as saying that from his experience, the IDF is the most moral army in the world.[20]

A PALESTINIAN HOMELAND?

In 1947, Great Britain relinquished its Mandate for Palestine. In 1921, Great Britain had been mandated, following the Balfour Declaration, the San Remo Peace Conference and the League of Nations, to provide a homeland for Jews in Israel; it gave away some 77 per cent of Israel's land, Transjordan, to the Palestinian Arabs, and the country of Jordan was created. It could be argued that there already is a Palestinian state and its name is Jordan. In 1947, the Peel Commission proposed dividing the remainder of the land to create an Arab state and a Jewish state. Israel said yes and the Arabs said no. When the state of Israel was established in 1948, each of the Arab and Islamic states refused to recognize its legitimacy. At present 32 United Nations member states refuse to recognize the state of Israel. Of the 22 members of the Arab league, 18 members refuse to recognize the state of Israel.[21]

There have been further offers of land for the remainder of the Palestinian Arabs (refugees). The Palestinians were offered 95 per cent of the West Bank (Judea and Samaria) in the year 2000 at the Camp David negotiations between prime minister Ehud Barak and PLO leader Yasser Arafat, but Arafat turned down the offer. Although the full details of the talks were never formally made public, it was reported in the media that the talks broke down over the status of Jerusalem.

Significantly, Yasser Arafat brought no proposals to the Camp David talks and was unable to make any concessions. This poor response apparently angered President Clinton. Later that year, in December, at the request of Yasser Arafat, the three leaders met again at the White House where President Clinton offered a final settlement. This offer was endorsed by Israeli prime minister Barak, but rejected by Arafat. This offer, never written down, but '... would have given the Palestinians 97 percent of the West Bank (either 96 percent of the West Bank and 1 percent from Israel proper or 94 percent from the West Bank and 3 percent from Israel proper), with no cantons, and full control of the Gaza Strip ...'[22]

That Israel should offer so much is hard to believe, but what is more difficult to believe is that on each occasion when the Palestinians have been offered land in Israel, they have turned it down! This would seem to indicate that the Israeli conflict is not a conflict over land, but an objection to any shared existence with the State of Israel.

ISRAEL IS REBORN AND FIGHTS FOR SURVIVAL

On 14 May 1948, following Great Britain's withdrawal from Palestine, Israel declared its independence, and the State of Israel was established after an exile lasting almost 2,000 years. Less than twenty-four hours later, five regular Arab armies from Egypt, Jordan, Syria, Lebanon and Iraq attacked the tiny population of Israel, determined to annihilate the Jewish state along with every Jew. These armies vastly outnumbered and outgunned the untrained civilian population of Israel. The war lasted fifteen months and the newly formed IDF managed to defeat the Arab armies with a loss of 6,000

Israeli lives, some 1 per cent of the population. Since this War of Independence, Israel has had to fight five defensive and at least five major terrorist attacks. The survival of the State of Israel is, by any standard, a miracle. Yet in spite of this, Israel survives to this day. Did you know that Israel is the only nation on the face of the earth that is guaranteed a future?

'For I am with you,' says the LORD, 'to save you; Though I make a full end of all nations where I have scattered you, Yet I will not make a complete end of you. But I will correct you in justice, And will not let you go altogether unpunished.'

(JEREMIAH 30:11)

'Thus says the LORD, Who gives the sun for a light by day, The ordinances of the moon and the stars for a light by night, Who disturbs the sea, And its waves roar (The LORD of hosts is His name): 'If those ordinances depart From before Me, says the LORD, Then the seed of Israel shall also cease from being a nation before Me forever.' Thus says the LORD: 'If heaven above can be measured, And the foundations of the earth searched out beneath, I will also cast off all the seed of Israel For all that they have done, says the LORD.'

(JEREMIAH 31:35–37)

WHO EXACTLY ARE THE PALESTINIANS?

Between 1882–1939, some 417,000 Jewish people escaping persecution in European nations, returned home to the land of Israel.[23] Working hard, they were able to reclaim the land and to make it fruitful. This made it attractive to the surrounding Arab peoples who migrated to Palestine, as it was then called, for economic reasons in order to benefit from the growing prosperity. Therefore, Palestinian Arabs are a disparate group of mainly Arab peoples from Arab nations. Before the Arab armies attacked Israel, which they did following Israel's declaration of independence on 14 May 1948, some 472–750,000 Arabs left what later became Israel (these figures are disputed by Arab scholars). Although present-day Palestinians are seeking statehood, bear in mind that the Palestinians have not lost a state that needs restoring. There has never been a sovereign Palestinian state that occupied part of Palestine. Their grandparents, or in some cases, their great-grandparents, are refugees from a conflict initiated by the five Arab nations mentioned above in order to annihilate the newly born State of Israel in 1948.

Following Israel's defeat of the Arab armies, some 160,000 Arabs who lived within the borders of Israel accepted Israel's offer of peace to become Israeli citizens. Not only so, but three Arabs were elected to the first Knesset.

Today, there are estimated to be 5 million Palestinian refugees.[24] The biggest percentage of these are the descendants of the original Palestinian refugees. How many original refugees were there? The figure is disputed but below is a quote from an Israel source.

The number of Palestinian Arabs who left, left what became Israel for several reasons:

- Most fled to escape the fighting, which Israel didn't start and didn't want.
- Wealthy classes fled to avoid the coming war. Without their leadership, Palestinian civil society fell apart, causing more flight.
- Many left because Arab leaders encouraged them to get out

of the way of advancing Arab armies, promising victory would be quick and they could soon return.

- Many left as Arab propaganda backfired when its manufactured tales of Israeli atrocities caused panic.
- In some cases, Israeli troops forced Arab residents from their homes in sensitive strategic zones vital to the survival of the young State of Israel.[25]

Do Arab leaders acknowledge these facts? Here are two interesting Arab quotes: 'The Arab armies entered Palestine to protect the Palestinians ... but instead they abandoned them, forced them to emigrate and to leave.' (Palestinian Authority president Mahmoud Abbas, 1976); 'We will smash the country. The Arabs should conduct their wives and children to safe areas until the fighting has died down.' (Iraqi prime minister Nuri Said, 1948) The demand for the now 4 million refugees is nothing more than a tactic to obliterate Israel. 'If Arabs return to Israel – Israel will cease to exist.' (Gamal Abdel Nasser, President of Egypt, 1961); 'The demand for the return of the Palestinian refugees ... is tantamount to the destruction of Israel' (As'ad Abd-Al Rahman, Palestinian Authority Minister of Refugee Affairs, 1999).[26]

Are the Palestinians badly treated? Yes, they have been, and still are, but by whom? By their Arabs brothers, who are rich in petrodollars, and whose land is huge compared to Israel – more than big enough to absorb them all, including all the descendants of the refugees. Notwithstanding, they have steadfastly refused the refugees entry, citizenship and jobs. The Palestinian refugees have been used as a political weapon against Israel, to the detriment of the Palestinians, since 1949.

It is worthy of mention that between 1948–54 some 850,000 Jews either fled or were expelled from Arab and Muslim lands. Although it was a struggle, Israel integrated some 600,000 Jewish refugees following the War of Independence. Today, Israel welcomes Jews from any country in the world. In these days God is calling Jews from every country where He has scattered them, to Israel. They are returning home from exile; this is a highly significant prophetic sign.[27]

UNDEMOCRATIC TREATMENT

Until recently, Israeli government ministers wishing to come to the UK ran the risk of being arrested on suspicion of having committed 'war crimes'. (Subsequently, at the request of Israel, the UK changed the law on 15 September 2011 to prevent private individuals being able to bring war crimes charges against Israeli officials visiting the United Kingdom.[28]) Sadly, there are Christians who are actively involved in supporting this vicious campaign. Having attended several Jewish meetings in London and witnessing the ant-Israeli hostility always present at a Jewish event, I am convinced that the BDS campaign is fuelled by anti-Semitism. Unfortunately for them, they are misinformed of the facts. If Arabs can become Israeli citizens and members of the Knesset and Israeli Arabs can vote in Israeli elections, it is hard to see how the accusation of an apartheid state, often levelled against Israel, can possibly be true. However, if the Palestinians are granted east Jerusalem as their capital, this will make the Palestinians themselves guilty of apartheid, as they have made it clear that no Jews would be allowed to enter or to live there. This is the declared intention of PLO president Mahmoud Abbas.[29]

Some argue that Israel's building of a security fence amounts to segregation. Those who take this view fail to value the lives of Israeli citizens. Israel was forced to build this fence in order to protect its citizens from suicide bomb attacks. A large part of the fence, some 96 per cent, is chain-link that utilises an early warning system. The remainder, some 4 per cent, is made of concrete. Before the security fence was erected, men, women and children were indiscriminately killed, including Arabs. Rockets are still fired over the fence, but it is a fact that many hundreds of lives have been saved since the fence was built. The border checks that Palestinians must undergo directly stems from Hamas operatives and other terrorist groups who are intent on murder, and would, if unchecked, be able to bypass security, thereby causing harm to innocent lives.

THEOLOGICAL ANTI-SEMITISM

It is not just amongst the nations of the world that anti-Semitism is being expressed. Surprisingly, there are Christian leaders who are anti-Israel and anti-Zionist in their theology. Zion is a central and recurrent theme in the Bible (Psalm 2:6; 9:11; 132:13; 135:21; 1 Peter 2:6; Revelation 14:1). A prime example of this is Christian Replacement Theology, which has received new life since 1967, when Israel recaptured east Jerusalem, Gaza and the West Bank. Fuelling all this is the doctrine that Israel has forfeited its right to the land of Israel, and that it is no longer relevant to the kingdom purposes of God.

A long time ago, the living God declared that cursing Abraham and his descendants would result in His curse being pronounced upon the guilty (Genesis 12:1–3; Numbers 24:9).

Anyone, whether they are Christian, atheist or humanist, who attempts to rob the Jewish people of their land or to divide their capital city, will be judged at the end of the age when He judges the nations (Joel 3:1–3; Matthew 25:31–46). These curses, mentioned in Genesis chapter 12, will be examined in what follows. In order to understand more fully the implications of all this, it is necessary to consider what God says about Israel – the land and its people. Let us begin by looking at a question that the apostle Paul asks in the book of Romans.

The Gentile believers in Rome asked Paul a very important question: 'I say then, has God cast away His people? Certainly not!' is his answer (Romans 11:1). Yahweh, the God of Abraham, Isaac and Jacob, describes Israel as: '... My son, My firstborn' (Exodus 4:22). The love that the Lord has for Israel is an everlasting love (Jeremiah 31:3). If there is one thing that we can be certain of, it is the faithfulness of the living God. He keeps covenant, and He will never completely abandon the Jewish people (Isaiah 49:14–16).

It is to our shame that we could ever think that God would abandon His firstborn son; yet, this is the teaching that pervades the Church – that Israel has been replaced by the Church in the affection of the Lord. In the Bible we shall discover that in this present age God has two covenant peoples – Israel and the Church – and He loves both.

WE ARE LIVING IN THE DAYS THAT THE PROPHETS SPOKE ABOUT
God is on the move. In spite of centuries of persecution and attempted genocide by their many enemies, the Jews have survived and remain a distinct people group. Israel is once more back in the land. Today the Jews are returning

from the nations where they have been scattered, to the Promised Land, Israel, their ancestral home. Essential to an understanding of God's purposes in the world in which we live is an understanding of the *aliyah*, which is the restoration of the Jewish people to the land of Israel and to their ancient capital, Jerusalem, in fulfilment of biblical prophecy. This is not an accident of history or an issue that can be ignored. This is nothing less than the trustworthiness of Scripture and the faithfulness of God to the glory of His great name:

> And I will sanctify My great name, which has been profaned among the nations, which you have profaned in their midst; and the nations shall know that I am the LORD,' says the Lord GOD, 'when I am hallowed in you before their eyes. For I will take you from among the nations, gather you out of all countries, and bring you into your own land. Then I will sprinkle clean water on you, and you shall be clean; I will cleanse you from all your filthiness and from all your idols. I will give you a new heart and put a new spirit within you; I will take the heart of stone out of your flesh and give you a heart of flesh. I will put My Spirit within you and cause you to walk in My statutes, and you will keep My judgments and do them. Then you shall dwell in the land that I gave to your fathers; you shall be My people, and I will be your God.'
>
> (EZEKIEL 36:23–28)

THE PROMISED LAND

The land of Israel is no bigger than the country of Wales and similar in size to New Jersey in the USA: a land given to Abraham and his descendants, the Jewish people, to dwell in by an everlasting and unbreakable covenant (Psalm 105:8–11). The land of Israel is also the land in which God has birthed His plan of salvation in His desire to bless both Jew and Gentile and to redeem the world (Genesis 12:1–3).

REVELATION AND CALL

I am grateful to the Lord for calling me to the ministry of Operation Exodus, which is the operating name of Ebenezer Emergency Fund International.[30] It has been a privilege to work with this significant end-time ministry for the last five years and to experience the joy of personally accompanying His covenant people on their return home to Israel, their ancient homeland. We are living in exciting days, when biblical prophecy is being fulfilled before our eyes. During my lifetime, we have seen the rebirth of the modern State of Israel after almost 2,000 years of exile. Since 1948, more than 3 million Jews from over 100 countries have returned home to Israel. They have come from the four corners of the world, including India and China. Today, the descendants of Abraham, Isaac and Jacob inhabit their ancient capital, Jerusalem. Not only so, but in spite of the many foreign languages spoken by these returning Jews, they are now speaking a modern version of their ancient Hebrew language. The restoration of the Hebrew language was the vision of one man, Eliazer Ben-Yehuda, who following arrival in Palestine in 1881 began to execute his plans for revival of the spoken language. Until his work, Hebrew was mainly a written language found only in religious texts, but was no longer used in everyday conversation. His aim was threefold: "Hebrew in the home", "Hebrew in the School", and, "Words, Words, Words"[31]. He is honoured today in Israel by having a street in Jerusalem named after him, Ben-Yehuda St. This is no accident of history. That the Hebrew language is being spoken today, after lying dormant since AD 135, is an exception compared to other ancient lost languages. It is my firm conviction that this is a miracle, a clear indication of the hand of the God of Abraham, Isaac and Jacob, the Almighty. The British mandate authority recognized the Hebrew language as the official language of Palestine on November 29, 1922[32].

For the largest part of my Christian life, I have taught and ministered to Gentiles. Not so long ago, as I was praying whether or not to accept an invitation to become UK chair of Ebenezer Emergency Fund,[33] the Lord said to me, 'I want you to help My people.' I knew instantly that He meant His Jewish people, so I said, 'Yes, Lord.' Since then the Lord has made me aware of the deep love He has for the descendants of Abraham '... I have loved you with an everlasting love; Therefore with loving-kindness I have drawn you' (Jeremiah 31:3). The descendants of Jacob are described as the apple of God's eye (Zechariah 2:8). The Bible teaches us that God's love is not sentimental; it is always based upon His righteousness that necessitates at times the discipline and judgement of those He loves. His love can never be extinguished, as it is everlasting (Hebrews 12:4–7).

Like most Gentile believers who read the Bible, my under-standing had been unknowingly darkened by the influence of the allegorical interpretation of Scripture taught by early Church fathers such as Augustine, Origen of Alexander and Justin Martyr. This view of Scripture has influenced the Church for many centuries and has become so ingrained that its presence is rarely discerned. This is an interpretation of Scripture that ignores the plain meaning of the words in their context and seeks a more 'spiritual' understanding. This spiritualising of the Scriptures has led to a number of distortions of Scripture, such as the false doctrine of Replacement Theology, sometimes called 'Supercessionism'.

If a passage of Scripture makes plain sense then we should seek no other sense! For example, when reading Scripture that refers to Israel and specifically to the house of Jacob, the common tendency is either to apply it to the Church or to fail to see it at all. Take as an example Luke 1:26–38 – The Annunciation. Believers with a high view of the inspiration of Scriptures have taken the plain meaning of Gabriel's message to Mary that she would supernaturally conceive and give birth to a Son and that His name would be Jesus. However, an essential part of Gabriel's message is missed. I refer to the following:

> He will be great, and will be called the Son of the Highest; and the Lord God will give Him the throne of His father David. And He will reign over the house of Jacob forever, and of His kingdom there will be no end.
>
> (LUKE 1:32,33)

Where was the throne of David? Was it in heaven or was it on the earth? It is an indisputable fact that David's throne was on the earth, and for the best part of his reign it was in Jerusalem. King David never had a throne in heaven! Whilst it is true that Jesus has ascended to heaven, He is not sitting upon the throne of his father David. This prophecy remains unfulfilled to this day. For Jesus to reign from the throne of His father David means He must return to this earth. Gabriel was very clear: He will reign over the house of Jacob from the throne of His father David. At this present time, and in this current age, Jesus occupies his Fathers throne, which is in heaven, and not upon the earth (Revelation 3: 21). The house of Jacob always means Jews and not Gentiles. If this message of Gabriel is to be fulfilled, then there have to be living descendants of Jacob dwelling in the land of Israel, with Jerusalem as their capital city. When we understand this, we see that the restoration of Israel as a nation is no accident of history, but an act of the living God. Realising this helps us to see the significance of the return of the Jews to the land of Israel. The day is coming when Israel as a nation will recognise that Jesus is their Messiah, and He will reign over them in Jerusalem (Ezekiel 36; Zechariah 14; Romans 11:26,27).

In recent years, a new expression of Replacement Theology has arisen called Fulfilment Theology.[34] According to Replacement Theology, the Church has replaced Israel. According to Fulfilment Theology, Jesus has replaced Israel. The name is different but the result is the same: Israel has been cast aside, and therefore God must have broken His promises to Abraham. This false and deceptive interpretation of the Bible teaches that God had rejected the Jews since the nation of Israel was complicit in the death of Christ, after they failed to recognise and proclaim Jesus of Nazareth as Israel's Messiah. This means that the scriptures that refer to the restoration of Israel as a nation, and the promise of a future kingdom to Israel (Acts 1:6) cannot possibly refer to the old Israel but now must be reinterpreted to mean the 'new Israel' – the Church! In their sermons, the Church fathers cursed the Jews and accused them of being 'Christ killers'[35] who consequently were destined to wander the earth, forever lost and under the curse of God.

So, according to Replacement Theology, the Church has now become the 'new Israel'. This means that all the unfulfilled promises and blessings given to Israel are now transferred to the Church. Like many believers, I had not consciously chosen to believe this teaching, but its pervasive influence on the interpretation of Scripture produced within me an inability to see the primary meaning and application of scriptures relating to Israel and a tendency to replace it with the Church as I fastened my belief on God's promises. This was an almost unconscious way of reading Scripture on my part. It was as if the Church had inherited all Israel's blessings, leaving Israel with only the curses as detailed in the Bible (Deuteronomy 28:15–68).

DECEPTION IN THE BODY OF CHRIST

This false teaching in the Church is one of the biggest barriers to a biblical understanding of Israel, hindering those who are interceding for the *aliyah* and seeking to enlist the support of fellow believers. Recently, this ancient heresy in its new form of Fulfilment Theology has arisen with considerable force advocated by some leading academic Christians such as Colin Chapman, author of *Whose Promised Land?*[36] Colin Chapman is lecturer in Islamic studies at the Near East School of Theology in Beirut. Stephen Sizer is the vicar of Christchurch in Virginia Water, UK. He is the author of *Christian Zionism; Road-map ro Armageddon?*, which is an attempt to refute biblical Zionism.[37] This viewpoint was supported by the influential Reverend John Stott who wrote the foreword to Stephen Sizer's book[38] Those who hold to this teaching deny that they are promoting Replacement Theology, but their teaching reaches the same conclusion: that the covenant made with Abraham, Isaac and their descendants sealed on oath by the eternal God has been modified and must now be transferred to the Church, as these promises have found their complete fulfilment in Jesus. The outcome of this false theology is that Israel, according to them, is now the same as any other nation and cannot claim eternally binding covenant promises such as their right to inherit and to live in the land of Israel. In their view, Israel as an elect nation is no longer relevant to God's purposes. Their role in bringing salvation to the world is now completed.

A further outcome of this teaching is that the *aliyah* is no longer necessary! This is one of the biggest barriers to the Church's understanding of the place of Israel in God's will and purposes. For a sound biblical analysis and refutation of Sizer's position, and all those who hold to the teaching of Replacement Theology and its close relative Fulfilment Theology, see Barry E. Horner's book: *Future Israel*.[39] See also Eliyahu Ben-Haim's booklet *Setting the Record Straight*, refuting the distortions in the popular documentary *With God on Our Side*.

To this day, many Church leaders believe that for a Jew to accept Jesus as their Messiah means that they must renounce their Jewish identity and all things Jewish. This is a completely unbiblical, deeply insulting and hurtful requirement (Romans 11:1). And to boldly state that Israel has no future as a nation directly refutes God's affirmation in Jeremiah 31 that Israel will be a nation before Him forever.

Thus says the LORD, Who gives the sun for a light by day, The ordinances of the moon and the stars for a light by night, Who disturbs the sea, And its waves roar (The LORD of hosts is His name): 'If those ordinances depart from before Me, says the LORD, Then the seed of Israel shall also cease From being a nation before Me forever.'

(JEREMIAH 31:35,36)

A PRAYER JOURNEY

This book was inspired by an Ebenezer prayer journey that I co-led in 2008 to Smolensk, a city about five hour's drive west of Moscow. It was a poor and dismal place. The invitation had come from Russian pastors who were concerned over their lack of unity and a sense that they were battling against some kind of curse. As they considered the possible cause of these spiritual difficulties, they realised that there was a history of severe anti-Semitism through the Russian pogroms and also by the German army on its march to Moscow during the Second World War, when many Jewish people were brutally murdered in huge numbers on Russian soil. It is generally overlooked that in the Ukraine from 1941–45, the Nazis murdered 1.5 million Jewish people.[40] A total of over 6 million Jews were murdered during the Second World War.

THE CRY OF SHED BLOOD

The Ebenezer leadership and representatives and I considered a prayer journey that would include praying at some of the sites where these atrocities had been carried out. Research was needed to discover the exact whereabouts of the sites, each having some kind of memorial to mark the evil events that took place there. These were places where Jewish people had suffered and been cruelly murdered; their blood had been spilled on the ground. Most readers will be aware of God's words following the murder of Abel:

> And He said, 'What have you done? The voice of your brother's blood cries out to Me from the ground. So now you are cursed from the earth, which has opened its mouth to receive your brother's blood from your hand.
>
> (GENESIS 4:10,11)

The time is coming when the earth will disclose the lives of all those whose blood has been shed. This includes Gentiles as well as Jews.

> For behold, the Lord comes out of His place To punish the inhabitants of the earth for their iniquity; The earth will also disclose her blood, And will no more cover her slain.
>
> (ISAIAH 26:21)

How much more will the Lord require an accounting for the blood of His firstborn sons and daughters (Exodus 4:23; Zechariah 2:8)? In preparation for this prayer action in Smolensk, I was able to draw on the principles in *Reclaiming the Ground*, in particular praying into the issues arising from the shedding of innocent blood. The journey began with a seminar for pastors and members of the prayer team. Chapter four includes this teaching on how to cleanse ground from the curse attached to the shedding of Jewish blood, providing helpful insights for those involved in praying for *aliyah*, which also entails prayer action to clear away the spiritual obstacles or stones:

Go through, Go through the gates! Prepare the way for the people; Build up, Build up the highway! Take out the stones, Lift up a banner for the peoples!

(ISAIAH 62:10)

It will also provide help for those who undertake prayer journeys. In many local churches there is lack of teaching on Israel, so it will be helpful to first consider Israel, its land and its place in God's will and purposes. This will enable us to better understand the spiritual consequences of anti-Semitism and how to seek the Lord for the removal of the curse attached to the shedding of Jewish blood, which is the evil fruit of anti-Semitism.

CHAPTER 2

THE SIGNIFICANCE OF ISRAEL AND CHRISTIAN ANTI-SEMITISM

THE DIFFERENCE BETWEEN ISRAEL AND THE NATIONS

The difference between Israel and the nations is the reason for Israel's rejection by the world. The people that form the nations of the world today are descendants from the three sons of Noah: Japheth, Ham and Shem (Genesis 10). The survivors of the worldwide flood were separated from each other following direct intervention from God when He confused their language at the Tower of Babel, after which they spread out over the whole earth, each people group being distinguished by their own individual language (Genesis 11:7).

The survivors from the flood had attempted to gain their independence from the living God; the building of the tower was the expression of their rebellion. This is probably one of the earliest manifestations of the spirit of religion and humanism, i.e. the exaltation and worship of humanity. It was at this time that God once again stepped into human history, and for His divine purposes revealed Himself to a man whom He had chosen to be the recipient of specific covenantal promises in order to bring about the salvation of humankind through Israel and its Messiah: God's Son, Yeshua Ha-Maschiach. The beginning of Israel as a people can be clearly traced to Abraham, a descendent of Shem, and his sons, Isaac and Jacob (Genesis 11:26).

SEPARATE FROM THE NATIONS

It was God's intention to create a people separate from the nations who would be a holy people unto Himself, a kingdom of priests (Exodus 19:6; Leviticus 20:24; Deuteronomy 7:6). They would be a people who would receive the true revelation of the living God and His majesty, His holiness and His power.

> He declares His word to Jacob, His statutes and His judgments to Israel. He has not dealt thus with any nation; and as for His judgments, they have not known them. Praise the LORD!'
>
> (PSALM 147:19,20)

They would demonstrate how humans should approach Him in praise and worship. The Lord chose the Jewish people for His own inheritance. For the Lord's portion is His people; Jacob is the place of His inheritance (Deuteronomy 32:9). This truth was proclaimed on the basis of His foreknowledge long before Abraham had any children (Genesis 17:5). Throughout their history, the Jewish people have been separate from the nations and have dwelt alone, not counting themselves among the nations (Numbers 23:9).

Abram, as he was then called, out of obedience to the Lord, turned his back on idolatry and left his home to travel to a land that he had never seen (Hebrews 11:8). This land, promised to Abraham and his descendants forever, was to become the cradle of salvation and blessing for the whole world. Israel was to be governed by the living God in contrast to the nations who were governed by human leaders who led their people in the worship of idols and sacrifice to demons (1 Kings 11:33; 1 Corinthians 10:20). History records that Israel has not found this unique relationship easy, and at times have wished to be like the other nations (1 Samuel 8:5–7).

> What you have in your mind shall never be, when you say, 'We will be like the Gentiles, like the families in other countries, serving wood and stone.
>
> (EZEKIEL 20:32)

THE CHOICE OF ISRAEL

The Bible is unlike any other book, religious or secular. It is the only book that accurately prophesies events that have not yet occurred. The authority of the Bible is secured by the fulfilment of these prophecies (Isaiah 41:21–23). Approximately a third of the Bible is predictive prophecy. It comes to us by way of a revelation from its Author, the living God, via the Holy Spirit (2 Samuel 23:2; 2 Peter 1:20,21; 1 Thessalonians 2:13). This book that believers recognise as the Word of God (Matthew 24:35) gives the reason why Israel is so special to God: because of His love for them and on account of the oath that He had sworn to Abraham, Isaac and Jacob, the patriarchs:

> Concerning the gospel they are enemies for your sake, but concerning the election they are beloved for the sake of the fathers. For the gifts and the calling of God are irrevocable.
>
> (ROMANS 11:28,29)

This verse makes it clear that they are still loved by their God, who chose them to be His people, in spite of the fact that many of the Jewish leaders failed to recognise and accept Jesus as their Messiah, the One who came in fulfilment of the Word of God, concerning which they were both recipients and guardians.

> I say then, has God cast away His people? Certainly not! For I also am an Israelite, of the seed of Abraham, of the tribe of Benjamin. God has not cast away His people whom He foreknew.
>
> (ROMANS 11:1,2A)

> The LORD did not set His love on you nor choose you because you were more in number than any other people, for you were the least of all peoples; but because the LORD loves you, and because He would keep the oath which He swore to your fathers, the LORD has brought you out with a mighty hand, and redeemed you from the house of bondage, from the hand of Pharaoh king of Egypt.
>
> (DEUTERONOMY 7:7,8)

ISRAEL: THE LAND

The land of Israel is one-sixth of 1 per cent the size of the Arab world and is inhabited by 6 million Israeli Jews compared to Middle Eastern Arabs and Muslims, who number 300 million. There are twenty-one Arab nations, and the combined land space of their territories is 650 times greater than the tiny nation of Israel.[41] Yet, despite its size, this is the most important plot of land upon the whole earth because of the way that it relates to God's plan of salvation. It has already been witness to the incarnation of the Son of God, His death and His resurrection, and one day will be the land to which He returns to rule and reign. According to the flesh and religious upbringing, Jesus is, of course, Jewish, and Israel is the land from which a Jewish Messiah will rule and reign over the whole earth, including Israel and the nations (Luke 1:33), from His capital city, Jerusalem (Acts 1:11, Zechariah 14:4; Psalm 29 102:21; Isaiah 2:3). The battle over who controls this city is fierce and will increase in intensity as the second coming of Jesus draws closer. Satan, who is behind those nations that desire Israel's destruction, will fight to the last in his attempt to annihilate the Jewish people in order to prevent the return of Jesus. The outcome, however, is certain: Satan and all his forces will be defeated (Joel 3:16; Psalm 2:1–6; Revelation 17:14; 20:7–10).

A SCATTERED PEOPLE

It is estimated that there are 14 million Jews worldwide out of which nearly 6 million live in Israel. This means at the time of writing that there are slightly more Jews living in the Diaspora than in Israel. This balance will shift within a few years. The term Diaspora refers to those Jewish people who have been scattered across the face of the earth as a consequence of the unfaithfulness of their forefathers to the God of Abraham, Isaac and Jacob, with whom they are joined by an everlasting covenant (Genesis 12:1–3, 15:18, 17:1–8;

35:11,12; Psalm 105:7–11). For 1,832 years, from AD 135 to 1948, the Jewish nation has been prevented from living in the land given to them by the Lord. For all these years, they had no status as a nation, and although their capital city was and still is Jerusalem, they could not live there. It was in the late nineteenth century that Jewish people began to return to the land. Although the land is theirs as an everlasting possession, the condition laid down by the Lord for inhabiting the land was pure worship and clean living according to the Law of Moses. Thus, defilement of the land through sin resulted in their forefathers' expulsion from it. However, God is faithful to His promise to return His people, and then He will cleanse them and give them a new heart:

> For I will take you from among the nations, gather you out of all countries, and bring you into your own land. Then I will sprinkle clean water on you, and you shall be clean; I will cleanse you from all your filthiness and from all your idols. I will give you a new heart and put a new spirit within you; I will take the heart of stone out of your flesh and give you a heart of flesh.
>
> (EZEKIEL 36:24–26)

THE ABRAHAMIC COVENANT

It is important to appreciate that the promise of the land is based upon the Abrahamic Covenant, which is an unconditional covenant (Genesis 15:9–21). The Mosaic Covenant is an example of a conditional covenant where obedience to the covenant is the condition of receiving God's blessings (Deuteronomy 28). No such requirements were attached to the land covenant. Abraham was not included in the enactment of the covenant recorded in Genesis 15. It was normal practice for two parties entering into a covenant to walk together between the separated parts of the sacrificed animals. In doing this they were pronouncing death to themselves if they were ever unfaithful to the covenant.

In Abraham's case, it was God alone who walked between the separated parts of the animals, as indicated by a burning oven and a smoking torch (Genesis 15:17). During the enactment of the covenant, Abraham was in a deep sleep (v. 12)! The promises to Abraham were sealed by the oath of God Himself; that is, He swore by His own name. He bound Himself by Himself to keep the promise. God never lies or fails to fulfil His promises (Hebrews 6:17; Numbers 23:19). Expulsion from the land was never a permanent situation. There was always the promise that God would bring them back in the last days from the nations where He had scattered them (Genesis 17:8; Leviticus 18:28; 26:44; Deuteronomy 4:1; Jeremiah 31:10).

THE COVENANT OF CIRCUMCISION

There are some who argue that the covenant of circumcision renders the Abrahamic Covenant conditional. Circumcision is mentioned in Genesis 17, and it is argued that this is nothing less than the adding of a condition to the Abrahamic Covenant, and that failure to practice circumcision renders the Abrahamic Covenant null and void. This is not so.

The covenant of circumcision mentioned in Genesis 17 is described by the Lord as '... a sign of the covenant between Me and you' (Genesis 17: 11). As someone has said, it is the seed organ, through which Abraham's descendants will be born, that is cut. It is a very personal reminder of the

41

covenant relationship between God and Israel. The Scripture clearly states that it is the individual male who does not circumcise himself or his male children who will be cut off (Genesis 17:14). This has no bearing whatsoever on the nation. Circumcision is described as an 'everlasting covenant' (Genesis 17:13, but this does not annul the unconditional nature' of the Abrahamic Covenant, Genesis 17:7). Having said this, it is worthy of note that the right of circumcision is still practised by Jews today, some 3,500 years after God gave this command to Abraham. In fact, the only time in history when the practice has momentarily stopped has been during times of Jewish persecution.

A TWENTIETH-CENTURY MIRACLE

The birth of the modern State of Israel on the 14 May 1948 is nothing short of a modern-day miracle. Those who question the authority of the Bible ought to take note of this (Isaiah 66:8). Furthermore, since defeating Arab nations in a defensive war in 1967, the descendants of Abraham, Isaac and Jacob, the Jewish people, have now returned to their capital city, Jerusalem. Not only are they back in the land and constituted as a nation, but also they are speaking the Hebrew language – a language that has actually been raised from the dead. These indisputable facts are not only a miracle, they are a wake-up call to Christians that we are moving closer to the return of Jesus. The return of the Jews to Israel is the fulfilment of Bible prophecy (Isaiah 11:10–12; Jeremiah 16:14,15).

It is important to remember that although the modern State of Israel is only sixty-five years old, the nation of Israel is some 3,500 years old. This historical fact is something that the anti-Israel lobby is seeking to discredit through the use of various techniques such as revisionism, which is the attempt to rewrite the facts of history. Not only have Palestinian 'scholars' denied that the Western Wall has any significance to Jewish people, but also they have wrongly asserted that Jesus was a 'Palestinian'. This twisting of history disregards the fact that archaeological evidence proves the pre-existence of the Jewish Temple on the site, and Jesus' human lineage in the genealogies of Matthew and Luke, testify to His Jewish roots. Furthermore, the term 'Palestine' was not even used until well over 150 years after the birth of Jesus. Its original usage pertained to anyone, Jew or Arab, living in Israel.[42]

Their armament includes false accusations against Israel, denial of the Holocaust, biased media reporting and the use of propaganda, which is the constant repetition of lies. The current campaign to de-legitimise and to demonise Israel, and the use of double standards in judging Israel, is a prime example, along with the boycott of Israeli goods.

These various means are successful because of the constant stream of pro-Palestinian propaganda, which the media accepts without knowledge of history or the verification of the facts.

MEDIA BIAS AND MISREPORTING

Sadly, some news channels do not accurately report events as they occur, or present them in context. Also, some newspapers have been found guilty by various media watchdogs of biased reporting and even anti-Semitism.

The language used in television or press reports gives an idea of the bias of the channel or newspaper, if not the journalist concerned. For example, when reporting on the Israel–Palestinian conflict, certain words represent specific political positions: 'Arab east Jerusalem'; 'illegal occupation'; 'disproportionate response'; 'against international law'; 'abuse of human rights'; 'apartheid state' – media reports contain an uncritical use of such words. Reports are often reinforced by visual images that show Israel in a bad and often false light.

There are a number of websites in the English-speaking world that monitor the accuracy of media reporting and seek to defend Israel from media bias (http://honestreporting. com/; CAMERA is the Committee for Accuracy in Middle East reporting in America http://www.camera.org/).

It is worth visiting official Israeli websites to verify the accuracy of an incident. Israel will always seek to verify the exact circumstances of any incident before they issue an official response:

Israel Ministry of Foreign Affairs: http://www.mfa.gov.il/ MFA;

Prime Minister's Office: http://www.pmo.gov.il/PMOEng;

Israeli Defence Forces: http://dover.idf.il/IDF/English/;

Knesset: http://www.knesset.gov.il/main/eng/home.asp.

Israel is highly self-critical, being a liberal democracy. This is not so with Arab or Palestinian sources. Journalists often find that after any serious incident, those who are against Israel have already prepared illustrated reports to save them time.

The language of these biased reports has become the language of governments' spokespeople. Consequently, many Western nations have criticised Israel for seeking to defend its citizens, by accusing them of 'disproportionate response'. Compared to the current situation in Egypt and Syria, Israel's response has been moderate, to say the least. Having said this, Israel's defence of its citizens can hardly be compared to the so-called 'Arab Spring', an internal fight for democracy, whereas Israel is a well-established democracy. According to the current widespread view, Israel should withdraw for the 'occupied territories', and if they did, there would be peace. Politicians and journalists are frequently heard using the term 'illegal settlements'. They seem unaware of the legal right established in international law that Israel has been granted the right to 'close settlement' in the land. This includes areas that have been wrongly described as 'occupied territories'; disputed territories would be more accurate.

These words can be heard from the lips of senior politicians. For example, on Wednesday, 8 February 2012 in committee room ten of the House of Commons, and in the author's presence, the chair of the Conservative Friends of Israel said that in his view, the 'occupied territories' were the main obstacle to peace.[43] It is, however, a fact of history that Israel has been granted legal entitlement to 'close settlement' of the land of Israel – and this includes east Jerusalem and the West Bank – guaranteed by the San Remo Conference, and later by the League of Nations, which became the United Nations, and this right is enshrined in international law. The San Remo Conference took place following the First World War in April 1920, and was attended by the prime ministers of Great Britain, France and Italy, and representatives of Japan, Greece and Belgium. It was at this time that the Ottoman Empire ceased to exist, and mandates were given to France and Great Britain over Syria, Lebanon, Iraq and Palestine, which in time became independent nations.[44]

This is a widely held view amongst those who ignore the Bible, God's Word, and are unaware of the facts of history.

If only Israel would withdraw from the so-called 'occupied territories', the conflict would end! Well, Israel withdrew from the Gaza Strip in August 2005. The response from Hamas was to indiscriminately fire over 8,000 rockets into Israel. It was not until 27 December 2008, some three years later, that Israel initiated Operation Cast Lead. For this defensive action, Israel was wrongly accused of war crimes, of purposely attacking and killing civilians, by a UN Fact Finding Mission led by Judge Richard Goldstone, in which his published report came to the following conclusion: 'The UN Fact Finding Mission finds strong evidence of war crimes and crimes against humanity committed during the Gaza conflict; and calls for end to impunity.'[45]

Judge Goldstone changed his judgement following further facts which subsequently came to light. Israel had refused to cooperate with the report, wishing to take the time to investigate the facts carefully. Therefore, Goldstone based his report on 'evidence' taken from Palestinians themselves, and Hamas terrorists. Below are extracts from an article he wrote for *aliyah* after the publication of his report.

> If I had known then what I know now, the Goldstone Report would have been a different document ... The allegations of intentionality by Israel were based on the deaths of and injuries to civilians in situations where our fact-finding mission had no evidence on which to draw any other reasonable conclusion ... the investigations published by the Israeli military and recognized in the U.N. committee's report indicate that civilians were not intentionally targeted as a matter of policy ...
>
> (JUDGE RICHARD GOLDSTONE, 2 APRIL 2011)[46]

Not only so, but Britain's foreign secretary William Hague's initial response to the Goldstone report was to say, 'Goldstone raised some important issues, which all concerned have to address. And of course democracies and free societies are held to high standards and should be.'[47] This statement implies that there may be truth in the UN report, which was subsequently found to be untrue as it was not based upon the facts.

Although claiming territory for the 'Palestinians', Yasser Arafat, who has been described as 'the father of modern terrorism' was, in reality, Muhammad Abdel Rahman Abdel Rauf al-Qudwa al-"Husseini and he was born in Egypt in 1929.[48] One of his weapons of choice against Israel was airplane highjacking. 'In 1969 there were eighty-two recorded hijack attempts worldwide, more than twice the total attempts for the whole period of 1947–67. Most were Palestinians using hijacks as a political weapon to publicise their cause and to force the Israeli government to release Palestinian prisoners from jail. Airliner hijackings have declined since the peak of 385 incidents between 1967–76. One of the most famous was the Palestinian hijack of the Air France Flight 193 airliner in 1976, which was brought to an end at Entebbe airport, Uganda, by Operation Entebbe: Israeli commandos assaulted the building holding the hijackers and hostages, killing all the Palestinian hijackers and freeing 105 mostly Israeli hostages; three passengers and one commando were killed'.[49]

Historically, Arab terrorism pre-dates the birth of the modern State of Israel in 1948. For example, Arab attacks against Israelis occurred as early as 1920, and of special note is the Hebron massacre that occurred on August 23–24 September 1929.[50]

WHOSE LAND IS IT, AND DOES IT REALLY MATTER?

The whole earth belongs to the living God who created it (Exodus 19:5) and everything in it (Psalm 50:12). The heavens are His (Deuteronomy 10:14). When God separated humankind into nations, the determining factor was the number of the sons of Israel:

> When the Most High divided their inheritance to the nations, When He separated the sons of Adam, He set the boundaries of the peoples According to the number of the children of Israel.
>
> (DEUTERONOMY 32:8)

The nations were given their inheritance, and God chose Israel's inheritance. Listen to what the Lord says: 'On that day I raised My hand in an oath to them, to bring them out of the land of Egypt into a land that I had searched out for them, "flowing with milk and honey," the glory of all lands' (Ezekiel 20:6). The Lord refers to this piece of land as His:

> The land shall not be sold permanently, for the land is Mine; for you are strangers and sojourners with Me.'
>
> (LEVITICUS 25:23)

The demand of the Palestinian Arabs and the whole of the Muslim world for a Palestinian state in the land of Israel with east Jerusalem as its capital is a direct challenge to the living God. It should be clear to every fair-minded person who follows world events that this demand is not accompanied by a desire to live in peace alongside Israel in the land, but a step towards the complete removal of the Jewish people from

Israel. For example, Yasser Arafat said to an Arab audience in Stockholm, Sweden, on 30 January 1996: 'You understand that we plan to eliminate the State of Israel and establish a purely Palestinian State. We will make life unbearable for Jews by psychological warfare and population explosion I have no use for Jews; they are and remain Jews.'[51]

Unfortunately for them, they harbour an ancient hatred of Israel. This claim, stemming from their religious ideology, is not grounded in history, international law or the Word of God. Furthermore, the word 'Jerusalem' does not even occur once in the Qur'an. Since 1948, Israel has been dragged into five major wars in order to defend its very existence.

- 1948 The War of Independence
- 1956 The Sinai War
- 1967 The Six Day War
- 1973 The Yom Kippur War
- 1982–85 The Lebanon War

It is their Islamic neighbours who have instigated these wars, with the sole intention of wiping Israel off the face of the earth. As noted above, the creation of Palestinian Arab refugees was the direct consequence of the failed attempt of five Arab armies to annihilate the newly formed State of Israel in 1948. Therefore, it is the Arabs and not the Jews who are responsible for the plight of these refugees. Since 1948, Israel has lived with the daily threat of attack, and throughout its long history many Jewish men, women and children have lost their lives as a consequence of anti-Semitism. Since Israel withdrew from Gaza in 2005, thousands of rockets have been indiscriminately fired by Hamas into the civilian population of Israel. Israel did not respond with military strikes until 27 December 2008, when the Israeli Air Force launched Operation Cast Lead, consisting initially of airstrikes and then later with ground forces. Much Jewish blood has been shed while Israel's enemies attempt to remove the Jews not only from their land but also from the face of the earth, so that they no longer exist as a people. For example, the Hamas charter contains the following principles:

'Israel will exist and will continue to exist until Islam will obliterate it, just as it obliterated others before it.' (The Martyr, Imam Hassan al-Banna, of blessed memory).

'There is no solution for the Palestinian question except through Jihad. Initiatives, proposals and international conferences are all a waste of time and vain endeavors'[52].

The above statements make it clear that the issue of land is not the real problem; it is the very existence of Israel. 'If the Arabs (Moslems) put down their weapons today there would be no more violence. If the Israelis put down their weapons today there would be no more Israel. Think about it ...'

(ANONYMOUS QUOTE)[53]

THE FEAR OF ISLAM

We are witnessing a worldwide increase in the influence of Islam. Although it is non-pc to say so, rather than bringing peace, the spread of Islam has resulted in an increase of Islamic fundamentalism. The term *Islamist* has been brought into common use and it refers to those Muslims who engage in *jihad* through acts of terror such as 'suicide bombing'.[54] It is a historical fact that Islam was established through bloodshedding. However, there is reluctance within the Church to identify the true nature of Islam. But it needs to be said that we do not worship the same God as the Muslims. Allah is not Yahweh. Furthermore, Islam denies that God the Father has a Son. It is important that in all friendly contacts with Muslims Christians are clear on this fact, and unwilling to compromise. A Muslim is unlikely to respect a Christian who avoids the clear differences between Islam and Christianity, and pretends that there is common agreement. Some may argue that not all Muslims are *jihadists*. Whilst this is true, it is worth bearing in mind that however nice and sincere the majority of Muslims are, they belong to a religion that promotes unquestionable obedience and encourages Muslims to 'liberate Palestine'. The following statement by the supreme leader of Iran was made during a meeting with hundreds of veterans from the Iraq–Iran war, 15 August 2012, by the supreme leader of Iran: 'Ayatollah Seyed Ali Khamenei ... noted that liberating Palestine from the grip of Israel and its allies is a religious duty for all Muslims across the world.'[55]

Islam even executes its own people who convert to Christianity. Not only so, but in Egypt, Sudan and Nigeria, just to name a few countries, Islamists are murdering Christians and burning churches. There is only one name through which humankind can obtain freedom from God's judgement against sin:Nor is there salvation in any other, for there is no other name under heaven given among men by which we must be saved' (Acts 4:12). His name is Jesus (see 1 Timothy 2:5).

One essential ingredient of Islam that should concern all

prayer warriors is the Arab and Muslim hatred of Israel and of the Jewish people. One only has to read the Qur'an to see how Muslims view Jews.[56] Having said this, we know that the Lord wishes to set the Muslim world free from such bitter hatred and bring them into salvation. We will not influence them by showing fear (Acts 4:13; 1 Peter 3:14; 2 Timothy 1:7). For one thing, anyone who seeks the annihilation of the Jews will not enter into God's blessings. Islam opposes the Jewish presence in the land of Israel and consequently is against the *aliyah*. Not only so, but Islam wrongly teaches that Ishmael and not Jacob is the inheritor of the land covenant promised to Abraham.[57] The Bible makes it clear that God's covenant was established with Isaac and not Ishmael.

'Then God said: 'No, Sarah your wife shall bear you a son, and you shall call his name Isaac; I will establish My covenant with him for an everlasting covenant, and with his descendants after him.

(GENESIS 17:19)

God did not leave Ishmael without a blessing:

And as for Ishmael, I have heard you. Behold, I have blessed him, and will make him fruitful, and will multiply him exceedingly. He shall beget twelve princes, and I will make him a great nation.

(GENESIS 17:20)

WHAT ABOUT THE PALESTINIANS?

The Palestinians are a mixed people group, although the majority are Arabs and are descended from the sons of

Ishmael. Ishmael fathered twelve princes or rulers who became the father of the different Arab tribes.

> These were the sons of Ishmael and these were their names, by their towns and their settlements, twelve princes according to their nations.
>
> (GENESIS 25:16)

Therefore, the Palestinians, being descendants of Ishmael, are inheritors of the blessing that God gave to Ishmael. The prophet Isaiah mentions that Israel and the Egyptians, along with Syria, will one day worship the God of Israel.

> In that day there will be a highway from Egypt to Assyria, and the Assyrian will come into Egypt and the Egyptian into Assyria, and the Egyptians will serve with the Assyrians. In that day Israel will be one of three with Egypt and Assyria – a blessing in the midst of the land, whom the LORD of hosts shall bless, saying, 'Blessed is Egypt My people, and Assyria the work of My hands, and Israel My inheritance.'
>
> (ISAIAH 19:23–25)

This is an amazing prophecy. Currently, Egypt and Assyria are opposed to Israel and are under the rule of Islam. However, according to this prophecy they will not remain so forever. This means that the day is coming when the power of Islam will be broken. As far as the present-day Palestinian Arabs are concerned, they have the same need of the salvation provided by the God of Abraham, Isaac and Jacob through His Son Jesus; therefore, we should pray for them as we also pray for Israel.

Palestinian children are taught in school to hate Jews and to esteem martyrdom.[58] Palestinian mothers are taught to rejoice when their children become suicide bombers.[59] Palestinian schoolbooks identify the whole of Israel as Palestinian land with no mention of Israel at all.[60] Israel is often accused of ethnic cleansing, but in fact the guilty party is clearly the Palestinian leadership.

HATRED OF ISRAEL

The Bible records two attempts to annihilate the Jewish people. It should be clear to all Bible believers that the arch enemy of Israel is none other that Satan, who is behind the world rulers who rage against the living God and His Son (Psalm 1; Isaiah 14; Ezekiel 28). The first attempt to destroy the nation of Israel was under Pharaoh, king of Egypt, when he ordered the midwives to kill all Jewish baby boys (Exodus 1:15). Had they done so, the Jews as a distinct people group would have ceased to exist. Jewish women would eventually have had no choice but to marry non-Jewish men. The second occasion was when the wicked Haman manipulated King Ahasuerus into making a decree that on a certain day all the Jews were to be killed (Esther 3:11,12). These wicked acts against the Jews brought down God's terrible judgement upon the nation of Egypt. First, there was the ten plagues, and then came the death of the firstborn. Lastly, Pharaoh and his army were drowned in the Red Sea (Exodus 13:15; 14: 28). Neither did Haman and his followers escape God's judgement, as Haman and his ten sons were hanged, and the Jews were enabled to kill all their would-be murderers (Esther 9:1–32).

As we will see later, history records the many attempts

of state and Church to get rid of the Jewish presence from their lands.

GOD'S JUDGEMENT

The claim of Islam to the land of Israel has no basis in the Bible. What is more, the Word of God makes it clear that the nations are to be judged on this very issue of dividing the land (Joel 3:1–3).

> Therefore thus says the Lord GOD: 'Surely I have spoken in My burning jealousy against the rest of the nations and against all Edom, who gave My land to themselves as a possession, with wholehearted joy and spiteful minds, in order to plunder its open country.'
>
> (EZEKIEL 36:5)

> I will also gather all nations, And bring them down to the Valley of Jehoshaphat; And I will enter into judgment with them there On account of My people, My heritage Israel, Whom they have scattered among the nations; They have also divided up My land.
>
> (JOEL 3:2)

As we witness the present turmoil in the nations, we can see that we are already beginning to experience God's judgement. The economies of the world are failing, leading to civil unrest in some nations. Political leaders who unite together in agreeing to divide the land of Israel need to take note of these words. The two-state solution favoured by the West today is not in accordance with God's Word. It is vital to comprehend that the will of God can never be overruled or thwarted. In the end, His will always prevails (Psalm 33:10,11). God is judging and will continue to judge those nations that favour an unbiblical solution to the conflict in the Middle East. Even Christians who would seek to rob Israel of its God-given inheritance by dividing the land are not safe from God's anger. One day the Messiah will rule the world from Israel's capital city Jerusalem:

'Yet I have set My King On My holy hill of Zion.'
'I will declare the decree: The LORD has said to Me, '"You are My Son, today I have begotten You.["']

(PSALM 2:6,7)

Who is this King? He is Jesus of Nazareth, the Son of God, and Israel's Messiah, whom the nation of Israel will recognise (Matthew 23:39; Zechariah 12:10). One day His feet will stand upon the Mount of Olives when He returns to reign over the earth and its inhabitants (Zechariah 14:3–9). It is often said, and sometimes by those who claim to be friends of Israel, that the main obstacle to peace in the Middle East is Jewish settlement in the land. For example, it is said that the so-called West Bank is territory that rightly belongs to the Palestinians. In reply to this, one of the most important questions that we can ask is this: Did the Lord make everlasting promises to Abraham, Isaac, Jacob and their descendants to give them the land of Israel in perpetuity? And if He did, is He able and willing to keep this promise? If He is unable, then He is not almighty; if He is unwilling, then He is guilty of breaking His Word. Both of these conclusions are not only unthinkable; they are simply not true (Numbers 23:19).

Some have wrongly argued that the Jews have forfeited

God's promises because of their sin. This would have been the case if the promises were dependent solely upon human obedience, but the promise of the land is not based on the Mosaic Covenant, which is a conditional covenant, but is based on the Abrahamic Covenant, which is an unconditional one, one that is dependent upon God Himself for its fulfilment (Hebrews 6:13). An unconditional covenant is characterised by 'I will', which occurs five times in just two verses (Genesis 12:2,3). God never forgets:

> He remembers His covenant forever, The word which He commanded, for a thousand generations[.]
>
> (PSALM 105:8)

THE ABRAHAMIC COVENANT

> Now the LORD said to Abram: 'Get out of your country, From your family And from your father's house, To a land that I will show you. I will make you a great nation; I will bless you and make your name great; And you shall be a blessing. I will bless those who bless you, And I will curse him who curses you; And in you all the families of the earth shall be blessed.'
>
> (GENESIS 12:1–3)

The promise is repeated to Abraham in Genesis 15:17–21; 17:3–8 and to his son Isaac and his grandson Jacob (Genesis 26:2–5; 28:10–15). The name of the living God is YHWH – Yahweh - meaning 'I am that I am' or 'I will be what I will be'. The name implies self-existent being (Exodus 6:3). Why would the Creator of heaven and earth and of everything

57

that lives and moves and has its being allow Himself to be referred to as: 'the God of your father, the God of Abraham, the God of Isaac and the God of Jacob'? (see Exodus 3:6,16; Matthew 22:32; Mark 12:26; Luke 20:37; Acts 3:13, 7:32). The answer is that He had personally revealed Himself to Abraham, his son and his grandson and had made specific promises to them. He has bound Himself by an everlasting covenant to Abraham and all of his descendants forever (Psalm 105:6–11; Jeremiah 31:35–37).

THE LAND COVENANT
God entered into an eternal covenant with Abraham and his descendants, the Jewish people, that they were to inherit the land of Canaan: a land that stretches 'from the river of Egypt to the great river, the River Euphrates' (see Genesis 15:18–21). This was to be an everlasting possession:

> He remembers his covenant forever, The word which He commanded, for a thousand generations, The covenant which He made with Abraham, and His oath to Isaac, And confirmed it to Jacob for a statute, To Israel as an everlasting covenant, Saying, 'To you I will give the land of Canaan As the allotment of your inheritance[.]'
>
> (PSALM 105:8–11)

ALIYAH: THE FULFILLING OF BIBLE PROPHECY
What is God doing today? One thing is certain; He is actively bringing home the scattered descendants of Israel from the four corners of the world (Isaiah 11:12). And this is in preparation for the return of His Son. And yet, the Christian Church seems largely unaware of this! The Scriptures speak of

a second exodus; the first was when He brought the children of Israel out of servitude in Egypt:

> 'Therefore, behold, the days are coming,' says the LORD, 'that they shall no longer say, 'As the LORD lives who brought up the children of Israel from the land of Egypt,' but, 'As the LORD lives who brought up and led the descendants of the house of Israel from the north country and from all the countries where I had driven them.' And they shall dwell in their own land.'
>
> (JEREMIAH 23:7,8)

This second exodus will be of such a magnitude that it will completely overshadow the exodus from Egypt in Jewish conversation.

> 'Therefore behold, the days are coming,' says the LORD, 'that it shall no more be said, 'The LORD lives who brought up the children of Israel from the land of Egypt,' but, 'The LORD lives who brought up the children of Israel from the land of the north and from all the lands where He had driven them.' For I will bring them back into their land which I gave to their fathers. Behold, I will send for many fishermen,' says the LORD, 'and they shall fish them; and afterward I will send for many hunters, and they shall hunt them from every mountain and every hill, and out of the holes of the rocks.'
>
> (JEREMIAH 16:14–16)

This immigration to Israel is described by the Jewish people as making. In the year 2009, there was a 17 per cent global increase in the number of Jews making *aliyah*. From the UK there was an increase of 34 per cent - 835 new immigrants, and from USA and Canada 17 per cent - 3,800 immigrants. From Eastern Europe, including the former Soviet Union, there was a 27 per cent increase. The God of Abraham, Isaac and Jacob is faithful to His Word (Numbers 23:19; Jeremiah 31:35,36).

> 'Hear the Word of the LORD, O nations, And declare it in the isles afar off, and say, 'He who scattered Israel will gather him, And keep him as a shepherd does his flock.'
>
> (JEREMIAH 31:10)

It is worth repeating, as it establishes God's prophetic word, that since 1948, when the State of Israel was established, over 3 million Jews from more than 100 countries have found their way home to Israel. In Israel today, there are 6 million Jews and 1.3 million Arab-Israeli citizens. In obedience to God, Christians have been involved in assisting this *aliyah* of Jews to Israel. One such Christian ministry is Operation Exodus (Ebenezer Emergency Fund International), founded by Swiss businessman Gustav Scheller and his wife, Elsa. The Lord raised this ministry up in 1991 as a prayer instrument in the hands of the Holy Spirit to intercede for the accomplishment of His will to bring the Jewish people home to Israel. Operation Exodus has helped 138,000 Jews make *aliyah* mostly from the former Soviet Union. Some have travelled by plane, but most have sailed on ships hired by Ebenezer.

THE NATURAL BRANCHES

Many Christians believe that when a Jewish person accepts Jesus as the Messiah of Israel, they have become one of us – a Christian. It is actually the other way around. Through faith in Jesus we have become 'fellow citizens with the saints and members of the household of God' (Ephesians 2:19). We are the wild shoots that have been grafted into the olive tree. We are warned not to be arrogant, as there remains the possibility that we, like some of them, may be broken off because of unbelief: 'For if God did not spare the natural branches, He may not spare you either' (Romans 11:17–21).

> For I do not desire, brethren, that you should be ignorant of this mystery, lest you should be wise in your own opinion, that blindness in part has happened to Israel until the fullness of the Gentiles has come in. And so all Israel will be saved, as it is written: 'The Deliverer will come out of Zion, And He will turn away ungodliness from Jacob; For this is My covenant with them, When I take away their sins.' Concerning the gospel they are enemies for your sake, but concerning the election they are beloved for the sake of the fathers. For the gifts and the calling of God are irrevocable. For as you were once disobedient to God, yet have now obtained mercy through their disobedience, even so these also have now been disobedient, that through the mercy shown you they also may obtain mercy. For God has committed them all to disobedience, that He might have mercy on all.
>
> (ROMANS 11:25–32)

The apostle Paul did not cease to be Jewish following his acceptance of Yeshua as Israel's Messiah (Romans 11:1; Acts 21:39; 22:3). And so Jewish followers of Yeshua today retain their Jewish identity.

THE CALL TO PRAYER AND ACTION

As believers, we are called to pray God's will into being (Matthew 6:10). Although, in the sovereign will of God this is bound to happen (Psalm 33:10,11; Isaiah 46:9–11), we should not be surprised at the opposition we will face from Satan in his attempt to prevent *aliyah* from taking place. God's purposes will always prevail in the end, but it will not be established without a fight and without prayer. We see this throughout Scripture and typified in the life of Daniel, who prayed for the end of the Babylonian captivity in accordance with God's Word (Daniel 9:19). When Daniel prayed, the Lord heard his prayer and sent an angel with a message, but it took the angel three weeks to reach Daniel with God's Word because he met with resistance from demonic principalities (Daniel 10:12–14). The powers of darkness had been aroused by the activity of an angel. There is no doubt that prayer based upon God's Word arouses the powers of darkness and leads to powerful demonic opposition in the heavenly realms.

JUDGEMENT TEMPERED WITH MERCY

Although it is a fact that Israel was driven out of the land because of their disobedience (Deuteronomy 28:15,63,64), God's judgement is designed to be restorative as well as punitive. Although God is love, He is also a God of righteousness. We are exhorted to consider both the goodness and severity of God (Romans 11:22). Although God's judgement upon Israel has been severe, it has been tempered by His mercy. The God who scattered them is the God who promised to bring them back from all the nations where they have been driven:

The LORD has appeared of old to me, saying: 'Yes, I have loved you with an everlasting love; Therefore with loving kindness I have drawn you. Again I will build you, and you shall be rebuilt, o virgin of Israel! You shall again be adorned with your tambourines, And shall go forth in the dances of those who rejoice ... Behold, I will bring them from the north country, And gather them from the ends of the earth, Among them the blind and the lame, The woman with child And the one who labors with child, together; A great throng shall return there ...'

(JEREMIAH 31:3,4,8–12)

COMFORT MY PEOPLE

The prophet Isaiah records God's declaration that He will comfort His people and that He will speak comfort to Jerusalem (Isaiah 40:1,2). When you take into consideration the many times that Jerusalem has been destroyed and its Jewish residents massacred, it is not surprising that the Word of God speaks of its need for comfort. In AD 70 Jerusalem was captured and ransacked by the Romans. According to Josephus, the Jewish historian, over 1,000,000 Jews were killed and the few survivors were driven from the land. In AD 135, following the Jewish Bar Kokhba revolt, most of the remaining Jewish population were expelled from the Holy Land by the emperor Hadrian and were scattered among the nations of the world. Jews were forbidden to enter Jerusalem, and the city was ploughed with a yoke of oxen. It was not until much later in 1967 that access to Jerusalem was restored following the defeat of the Arab attacking armies after a time span of 1,832 years.

It was in AD 135 that the name of Jerusalem was changed to

'Aelia Capitalina' and the land of Israel was changed to 'Syria Palestina' (Palestine) after the Philistines, an ancient enemy of Israel that had disappeared from world history more than 600 years earlier. This is the origin of the designation 'Palestine'. This name change by the Roman emperor Hadrian was to further humiliate the Jewish people by robbing them of their national identity arising from the name of their historic capital city in their ancestral home.

At that time in history, and until after the rebirth of the modern State of Israel, both Arabs and Jews were described as Palestinians, as Palestine was simply the designation for a geographical area of the Middle East. Jewish people began returning to their homeland, the first *aliyah*, in 1882, after almost 1,900 years of exile, leading eventually to the establishment of the State of Israel on 14 May 1948.

THE HISTORY OF THE CHURCH AND ISRAEL

Those of us who have a Christian education through Sunday school and church have been taught to revere the heroes of the Bible: Abraham, Moses, David, Daniel, Gideon, Esther etc. But we have also been taught about Israel's sins: its idolatry, immorality, unfaithfulness, rebellion and hypocrisy. Most Christians have a positive image of Israel in the Bible, but modern-day Israel is seen in a less favourable light. For many Christians, present-day Israel has no significance. In some measure this is due to the misreporting and bias of the media. Consequently Israel is seen as the aggressor rather than as a state defending its people.

For any who would condemn Israel for its sins, let them first consider the history of the Church. At its birth on the day of Pentecost, the Church was entirely composed of Jews.

It was not until Acts chapter 10 that Gentiles were added to the 'commonwealth of Israel' (Ephesians 2:12). Not long after the founding of the Church to the day in which we live, the same sins – idolatry, immorality, unfaithfulness, rebellion and hypocrisy – are present within the body of Christ! Furthermore, we Gentile believers have sinned with much more of God's grace than the sons of Jacob. We have the indwelling Holy Spirit, the complete revelation of Scripture, the gifts of the Holy Spirit and immediate access to the Father through the shed blood of His Son.

CHRISTIAN ANTI-SEMITISM

If we take the time to learn the history of Christian anti-Semitism from the early Church to this day, it will produce within us feelings of shock, horror and revulsion. When we consider the words of Jesus recorded in Matthew chapter 25, how can we fail to open our hearts to our Jewish brother and sisters? Remember the words of Jesus: 'Assuredly, I say to you, inasmuch as you did it to one of the least of these My brethren, you did it to Me' and 'Assuredly, I say to you, inasmuch as you did not do it to one of the least of these, you did not do it to Me.' The brothers of Jesus include the Jewish people and those from among the Gentiles who have turned to Christ for their salvation, i.e. the disciples of Jesus Christ (Mark 3:34).

THE CRUSADES

The 'Christian' Crusades of the eleventh, twelfth and thirteenth centuries were attempts to liberate the Holy Land from Muslim control. The Church of the time mistakenly believed that the Holy Land belonged to Christians.

Christian soldiers were sent by the Pope to fight against Muslims, many of whom were slaughtered. Because of a false theology –Replacement Theology – Jews were also seen as the enemies of Christ and were slaughtered along with the Muslims. One such atrocity against the Jews occurred during the first crusade in 1099. Jews were rounded up and locked in a synagogue. Then the Crusaders set fire to it.[61] This was a horrific atrocity that bore no resemblance to the real Jesus, His teachings or His followers.

History records many similar acts against Jewish people done in the name of Christ. Christians are not exempt from the conditions of blessing and curse pronounced by the Lord in our treatment of His ancient covenant people (Genesis 12:1–3). The history of the Christian Church is stained with the blood of each Jew that has been killed in the mistaken belief that it was God's will to kill the Jews. God says that those who harm the people of Israel are touching the apple of His eye (Zechariah 2:8). It makes no sense for those who are grafted in to the Commonwealth of Israel to destroy the very root that supports them (Romans 11:16–18).

THE PROTESTANT REFORMATION

It is not widely known that Martin Luther, the great German reformer and father of the modern German language, expressed real hatred towards the Jews at the end of his life. In 1543 he wrote a pamphlet entitled *Von den Jueden und Ihren Lugen* (On the Jews and Their Lies). In this tract he lists seven pieces of advice as to how Christians should treat Jewish people.[62] Because of Luther's statements on what should be done with the Jews, the Nazis revered Martin Luther. According to some accounts, one of the Nazis, Julius

Streicher, referred to this tract in his defence at the Nuremberg I.M.T (International Military Tribunal), His words were: "Dr. Martin Luther would very probably sit in my place in the defendants' dock today if this book had been taken into consideration by the Prosecution[63]'

First to set fire to their synagogues or schools and to bury and cover with dirt whatever will not burn, so that no man will ever again see a stone or cinder of them. This is to be done in honor of our Lord and of Christendom, so that God might see that we are Christians, and do not condone or knowingly tolerate such public lying, cursing, and blaspheming of his Son and of his Christians. For whatever we tolerated in the past unknowingly – and I myself was unaware of it – will be pardoned by God. But if we, now that we are informed, were to protect and shield such a house for the Jews, existing right before our very nose, in which they lie about, blaspheme, curse, vilify, and defame Christ and us (as was heard above), it would be the same as if we were doing all this and even worse ourselves, as we very well know.

Second, I advise that their houses also be razed and destroyed ...

Third, I advise that all their prayer books and Talmudic writings, in which such idolatry, lies, cursing and blasphemy are taught, be taken from them ...

Fourth, I advise that their rabbis be forbidden to teach henceforth on pain of loss of life and limb.

Fifth, I advise that safe-conduct on the highways be abolished

completely for the Jews. For they have no business in the countryside, since they are not lords, officials, tradesmen, or the like.
Let they stay at home ...

Sixth, I advise that usury be prohibited to them, and that all cash and treasure of silver and gold be taken from them and put aside for safekeeping. The reason for such a measure is that, as said above, they have no other means of earning a livelihood than usury, and by it they have stolen and robbed from us all they possess ...

Seventh, I commend putting a flail, an axe, a hoe, a spade, a distaff, or a spindle into the hands of young, strong Jews and Jewesses and letting them earn their bread in the sweat of their brow, as was imposed on the children of Adam (Genesis 3:19). For it is not fitting that they should let us accursed Goyim toil in the sweat of our faces while they, the holy people, idle away their time behind the stove, feasting and farting, and on top of all, boasting blasphemously of their lordship over the Christians by means of our sweat. No, one should toss out these lazy rogues by the seat of their pants.

I imagine that most readers will be surprised and shocked by these terrible words. In this evil tract, Martin Luther, never a man to mince words, reinforces his advice as he continues his tirade against the Jews:

Accordingly, it must and dare not be considered a trifling matter but a most serious one to seek counsel against this and to save our souls from the Jews, that is, from the devil and from eternal death. My advice, as I said earlier, is:

First, that their synagogues be burned down, and that all who are able toss in sulphur and pitch; it would be good if someone could also throw in some hellfire. That would demonstrate to God our serious resolve and be evidence to all the world that it was in ignorance that we tolerated such houses, in which the Jews have reviled God, our dear Creator and Father, and his Son most shamefully up till now but that we have now given them their due reward.

How the great reformer could ignore the plain words of Scripture is beyond me: 'I say then, has God cast away His people? Certainly not! For I also am an Israelite, of the seed of Abraham, of the tribe of Benjamin. God has not cast away His people whom He foreknew' (Romans 11:1). That such a great man could speak in such a shameful manner indicates the power of deception. However, Martin Luther was not saying anything that the Church had not already stated in the sermons and writings of the early Church fathers between AD 100–600. Below are some of their sayings:

Ignatius, Bishop of Antioch, martyred AD 117: 'If anyone celebrates the Passover along with the Jews, or receives the emblems of their feasts, he is a partaker with those who killed the Lord and His Apostles.'[64]
Gregory Nyssa (died AD 394): 'They are the companions of the devil, they are a race of vipers, informers, culminators, darkeners of the mind, Pharisaic leaven and a Sanhedrin of

demons accursed, detested, lapidators, enemies of all that is beautiful.'[65]

John Chrysostom (AD 345–405) – 'John the Golden Mouth': He accused the Jews of eating their children and went on to say that they were: 'Lustful, rapacious, greedy, perfidious, bandits... inveterate murderers, destroyers, men possessed by the devil... debauchery, drunkenness has given them the manners of a pig, and a lusty goat.' 'God has always hated the Jews, [and] it is incumbent upon all Christians to hate the Jews.' (Hated the Jews? No, Scripture says, 'Yes, I have loved you with an everlasting love', Jeremiah 31:3.) 'It is because you killed the Christ, it is because you stretched out your hand against the Lord. It is because you shed his precious blood, that there is no restoration, no mercy any more, and no defence.'[66]

I realise that these words are shocking and deeply offensive. They are certainly contrary to Scripture. The fact is that it was the Romans who put Him to death. The cry 'Crucify Him' was not representative of every Jewish person, but the crowd that was present in Jerusalem at that time. The Word of God is clear. It was the chief priests who had stirred up the crowd (Mark 15:11–13). Even then, Jesus forgave them moments before He died, as they did not fully understand what they were doing (Luke 23:34). Jesus died for the sins of the world, your sin and my sin, and He laid down His life willingly; no one took it from Him, as He had the power to lay it down and then to take it again (John 3:16; 10:17).

Although the Scriptures are clear, the views that many early Church fathers expressed have poisoned the mind of Christians throughout the centuries, leaving behind a corrupt legacy. The assumption that God has finished with the Jews is widely believed among Christians in the twenty-first century. Luther's Reformation did nothing to restore the Jews to their rightful place in God's will and purposes. One can say without fear of exaggeration that such a distorted view of the Jews expressed through the many Christian pronouncements against them were in large part what led a Christian nation such as Germany to behave in the way that it did, first in passing legislation that removed from the Jews their rights and protection as citizens, and then in the mobilisation of its massive state machinery in pursuit of its policy to completely annihilate all Jewish people, young and old.

GENTILE RESPONSIBILITY AND GOD'S CALL TO THE NATIONS

We owe the Jewish brothers and sisters of Jesus a debt of love, not least because of the many spiritual blessings we have received through them, especially the blessing of a Jewish Saviour (Romans 15:27). Furthermore, we have received a call from God through His prophets to assist Him in bringing back His first covenant people from the nations where they have been scattered:

> Thus says the Lord GOD: 'Behold, I will lift My hand in an oath to the nations, And set up My standard for the peoples; They shall bring your sons in their arms, And your daughters shall be carried on their shoulders'
>
> (ISAIAH 49:22).

> 'Who are these who fly like a cloud, And like doves to their roosts? Surely the coastlands shall wait for Me; And the ships of Tarshish will come first, To bring your sons from afar, Their

silver and their gold with them, To the name of the LORD your God, And to the Holy One of Israel, Because He has glorified you. The sons of foreigners shall build up your walls, And their kings shall minister to you; For in My wrath I struck you, But in My favor I have had mercy on you. Therefore your gates shall be open continually; They shall not be shut day or night, That men may bring to you the wealth of the Gentiles, And their kings in procession. For the nation and kingdom which will not serve you shall perish, And those nations shall be utterly ruined.'

(ISAIAH 60:8–12)

Will we heed this call? If not, how will we face Jesus if we do nothing to help His people? We must prepare ourselves if necessary to suffer with them, which in practical terms means standing up for Israel, protecting them from the evils of anti-Semitism, visiting them in prison, feeding and clothing them.

CHAPTER 3

THE CURSE OF ANTI-SEMITISM AND ITS CONSEQUENCES

INTRODUCTION

In spite of the Holocaust and the many defensive wars Israel has had to fight for its existence, many Christians are indifferent or unsympathetic to the plight of the Jewish people. May I ask you a very important question: where do you stand on Israel? Are you sympathetic or critical? Before we begin to define the nature and consequences of anti-Semitism, I would like to share some facts that will test where our hearts are. It may be that our feelings towards Israel may change after we have considered these facts, both historical and biblical. What kind of thoughts and feelings does the following information produce in you?

HISTORICAL FACTS

In this, the twenty-first century, the media portrays Israel as the aggressor rather than the victim. We are led to believe that Israel is at fault for defending itself from those who would, if they could, annihilate Israel as a nation. Israel is portrayed by the media as the cause of the suffering of the Palestinian Arab people. At this point it will be helpful to ask, who was responsible for creating the Palestinian Arab refugees? We have already discussed this, but let us state it again. The creation of Palestinian Arab refugees was the result of several Arab nations losing a war that they themselves started in an attempt to annihilate Israel in 1948. It is they who have refused to absorb these, their own refugees. It is worth repeating that the land of Israel is one-sixth of 1 per cent the size of Arab lands, which own 99 per cent of the land that comprises the Middle East. Furthermore, Arab nations are rich in petrodollars. It is either unknown or conveniently forgotten that when Israel won the War of Independence in 1949, a war it fought for its existence, an equal number of Jewish refugees were created, being evicted from the surrounding Arab lands in which they had lived for hundreds of years. Prior to starting the war with Israel, the Arabs had been offered a Palestinian state in 1947 by the UN, which they flatly refused, as it would have meant recognising the State of Israel. Their response was to initiate war against Israel within twenty-four hours following Israel's declaration of Independence.

Yes, the Palestinians have been treated badly, but not by the nation of Israel. Between 1967–95, before Israel withdrew from Gaza, Israel built seven universities, twenty community colleges, and 166 clinics for the Palestinians. Many Christians are unaware of these facts and of the history of the conflict, not least because they glean their understanding of Israel from biased, inaccurate and incomplete media reports, which fail to report facts that are supportive of Israel. Israel has done more for the Palestinian people than their Arab brothers who have consistently refused them entry into their own nations. Before the war in 1948, Jewish leaders pleaded with their Arab residents to stay. In fact, the residents were told to go by the Arab High Council with the promise that once the Arab nations had destroyed the nascent State of Israel, they could return and would be able to occupy the entire land of Israel. Following the defeat of the invading Arab armies, Palestinian Arabs were invited by Israel to become Israeli citizens with equal rights alongside Jewish people. Some 166,000 Arabs accepted this very generous offer.

ISRAEL: THE ONLY MIDDLE EASTERN DEMOCRACY

According to the Israel Ministry of Foreign Affairs, the 2010 population of Israel was 8,081,000[67]. Within this number are approximately 1.3 million Israeli-Arabs.[68]. Not only do they have the vote, but also they are allowed their own political parties, and can become members of the Knesset, the Israeli parliament. There are currently five Israeli-Arab parties and they have held as many as twelve out of 120 Knesset seats won in a single election. These statements can be verified by checking the facts. Indeed, Israeli-Arabs can hold high office in Israel: Salim Jurban was selected in 2004 as a permanent member of Israel's Supreme Court; Major General Hussain Fares was appointed commander of Israel's border police. Arabic is an official language in Israel on a par with Hebrew. Israel recognises fifteen different religions.[69] Israel is the only Middle Eastern country where Christianity is thriving. Compare this with Saudi Arabia, Pakistan and other Islamic countries, where it can be almost impossible to build a church, and the punishment for conversion to Christianity is death.

How did you react?

Let us now consider the nature of anti-Semitism before examining the consequences.

ANTI-SEMITISM: A DEFINITION

Our first definition is a biblical and theological one provided by Fred Wright:

> The dynamic of anti-Semitism is the spirit of Antichrist, which is best understood as the spirit of anti-salvation. Fallen man cannot bear to be reminded of God and His responsibilities towards Him. As man cannot kill, dethrone, or physically remove or destroy Him, he attempts to remove the evidence of His existence. The desire may only be achieved by the removal of the physical evidence, namely the Jewish people.[70]

A wider definition of anti-Semitism can be obtained from the Stephen Roth Institute for Anti-Semitism and Racism based at Tel Aviv University. Two authors from the TAU, Dina Porat and Ken Stern have defined anti-Semitism and its outworking in the following way:

> Yet, without overly pushing the matter of anti-Zionism as anti-Semitism, a good working definition of anti-Semitism for monitors and incident counters might be the following, developed by this author along with other experts during the second half of 2004:
>
> Anti-Semitism is hatred toward Jews because they are Jews and is directed toward the Jewish religion and Jews individually or collectively. More recently, anti-Semitism has been manifested in the demonization of the State of Israel.

Anti-Semitism frequently charges Jews with conspiring to harm humanity, and it is often used to blame Jews for 'why things go wrong.' It is expressed in speech, writing, visual forms and action, and employs sinister stereotypes and negative character traits.

Contemporary examples of anti-Semitism in public life, the media, schools, and the workplace and in the religious sphere include, but are not limited to:

- Calling for, aiding, or justifying the killing or harming of Jews in the name of a radical ideology or an extremist view of religion.
- Making mendacious, dehumanizing, demonizing, or stereotypical allegations about Jews – such as, especially but not exclusively, the myth about a world Jewish conspiracy or of Jews controlling the media, economy, government or other societal institutions.
- Accusing Jews as a people of being responsible for real or imagined wrongdoing committed by a single Jewish person or group, or even for acts committed by non-Jews.
- Denying the fact, scope, mechanisms (e.g. gas chambers) or intentionality of the genocide of the Jewish people at the hands of National Socialist Germany and its supporters and accomplices during World War II (the Holocaust).
- Accusing the Jews as a people, or Israel as a state, of inventing or exaggerating the Holocaust.
- Accusing Jewish citizens of being more loyal to Israel, or to the alleged priorities of Jews worldwide, than to the interests of their own nations.

Examples of the ways in which anti-Semitism manifests itself with regard to the State of Israel include:

- Denying the Jewish people their right to self-determination, e.g., by claiming that the existence of the State of Israel is a racist endeavor.

- Applying double standards by requiring of it behavior not expected or demanded of any other democratic nation.
- Using the symbols and images associated with classic anti-Semitism (e.g., claims of Jews killing Jesus or blood libel) to characterize Israel or Israelis.
- Drawing comparisons between contemporary Israeli policy and that of the Nazis.
- Holding Jews collectively responsible for actions of the State of Israel.

However, it is worth pointing out that criticism of the policies of the Israeli government similar to that leveled against any other democratically elected government should not be regarded as anti-Semitic.

Anti-Semitic acts are criminal when they are so defined by law, for example, denial of the Holocaust or distribution of anti-Semitic materials in some countries, such as Germany and Austria. Criminal acts are anti-Semitic when the targets of attacks, irrespective of people or property – such as buildings, schools, places of worship and cemeteries – are selected because they are, or are perceived to be, Jewish or linked to Jews. Anti-Semitic discrimination is denying Jews opportunities or services available to others and is illegal in many countries.[71]

VIOLENT ATTACKS AGAINST JEWISH PEOPLE

The Stephen Roth Institute for the Study of Anti-Semitism and Racism based at Tel Aviv University define a major violent manifestation as: '... Major violent attacks such as arson, weapon attacks, weapon less attacks. Harassment, and vandalism or desecration.' The record of anti-Semitic incidents provided by this university is shocking.[72] For example: According to TAU criteria and data, the highest number of major violent manifestations recorded in 2010 were in the UK, France and Canada. The UK heads the table with 144 incidents, followed by France with 134 and Canada with 99. These statistics amounted to about 60 per cent of all incidents worldwide. 'The level of violent incidents, particularly physical assaults, remained very high in these countries even compared to 2009.' For the year 2010 worldwide there were 614 such attacks compared with only 78 in 1989.[73]

THE SPIRITUAL CONSEQUENCES OF ANTI-SEMITISM: I WILL CURSE HIM WHO CURSES YOU

These scriptures reveal God's framework for dealing with people and nations according to their treatment of Israel (Genesis 12:1–3; Numbers 24:9; Joel 3:1–3; Matthew 25:31–46). The first covenant was made with Noah (Genesis 9:8). The second covenant, eternal and unconditional, recorded in the Bible, is the one God made with Abraham, referred to as the Abrahamic Covenant. God called Abram and promised him that He would make him into a great nation, that He would bless him and through him would bless all the families of the earth. Bearing in mind that Abraham, and therefore Israel, is God's chosen instrument to bless the whole world, it is not surprising that God added He would curse anyone who cursed him:

Now the LORD had said to Abram: 'Get out of your country, From your family And from your father's house, To a land that

I will show you. I will make you a great nation; I will bless you
And make your name great; And you shall be a blessing. I will
bless those who bless you, And I will curse him who curses
you; And in you all the families of the earth shall be blessed.'

(GENESIS 12:1–3)

To curse Abraham and the nation that he would father is a
failure to recognise God's heart, His will and His purposes for
and through Israel, and is to set oneself against God Himself.
Anti-Semitism is not just hatred of the Jew; it is also hatred
of the God of the Jews.

God's intention for Abraham and his descendants,
Israel, is strengthened in its significance and importance by
declaring that not only does He desire to bless Abram and his
descendants, but it is His will that every other nation should
also bless them. If only nations today understood that the
key to experiencing God's blessing upon their people is to
bless Israel. There are many Christians praying for revival
who are oblivious to this major revival key. If the Church
were to bless Israel in accordance with God's Word, they
would experience tremendous blessing. As noted above, the
direct consequence of cursing the Jewish people is to bring
the individual or nation under a curse from God Himself.

NATIONS HAVE BEEN JUDGED BY GOD BECAUSE OF THEIR TREATMENT OF ISRAEL

History reveals a long list of ancient and modern nations
along with their leaders who have attempted to destroy Israel.
God never forgets His covenant promises or His judgements.
An ancient enemy of Israel was Amalek, who fought against
Israel at Rephadim as the Israelites were journeying through

the wilderness (Exodus 17:8–16). God's judgement against the Amalekites was severe. Not only would He blot out the remembrance of Amalek under heaven, but He would have war with Amalek from generation to generation (Exodus 17:16). The descendants of Ammon and Moab were not allowed to enter the assembly of the Lord because they did not meet the Israelites with bread and water when they came out of Egypt. They also hired Balaam to curse the children of Israel (Deuteronomy 23:3–6).

Look at the destruction that the hardhearted Egyptian pharaoh brought upon his own people and land because of his refusal to let the children of Israel go. Moreover, the Jewish Feast of Purim celebrates a victory for the Jewish people against another enemy, the wicked Haman the Agagite, possibly a descendant of Amalek, who was hanged on his own gallows that he had built for the Jew Mordecai. Why is it that great empires such as Egypt, Babylon, Media and Persia, Greece, Rome, Spain and the Third Reich have risen and then fallen or ceased to exist? What happened to the British Empire? It is a historical fact that Britain failed in its obligation to Israel under the terms of the British Mandate for Palestine by giving away over 74 per cent of the land allotted to Israel. It is hard to escape the conclusion that empires are judged on the basis of their treatment of Israel (Joel 3:1–3).

ATTACKS AGAINST THE JEWISH PEOPLE

When it comes to attacks against Jewish people, the Roman Catholic and Protestant churches have a diabolical record: the Crusades, the Spanish Inquisition, the Russian pogroms and the German Holocaust. Hardly a century has passed without brutal and cruel attacks against Jewish people. History testifies to the fact that those nations and their leaders who have attempted to destroy the Jewish people have themselves been severely punished or even completely destroyed; they have brought themselves directly under God's curse. Hitler's attempt to build a 1,000-year kingdom, the Third Reich, lies in the ashes of the Berlin bunker where he committed suicide. Judgement has fallen upon the once great USSR that refused to let Jews to Israel. This once mighty Communist empire has been humiliated and has lost control over its former domain.

THE DEMISE OF THE BRITISH EMPIRE

Great Britain was instrumental in the establishment of the State of Israel through the Balfour Declaration. Unfortunately, British policy changed dramatically. According to Derek Prince, who lived in Palestine at the time of Jewish Independence, the British military government did everything short of war to prevent the State of Israel from coming into existence. Those who take God's Word seriously will not find it difficult to trace the loss of the British Empire to Great Britain's harsh and brutal treatment of the Jewish people. Britain restricted Jewish immigration to Palestine in 1939, and as a consequence, many Jews who could have fled Nazi persecution lost a vital means of escape. Britain treated them as illegal immigrants; they maintained this policy throughout the war.

In spite of the horrors of the Second World War, the British forced the surviving Jews to remain in the concentration camps and sank boats that tried to reach the coast of Palestine illegally. Those Jews who did not drown but managed to swim ashore were picked up by the British and placed in new concentration camps in Cyprus. Patriotic Jews in Palestine were hung.[74]

THE CHURCH AND ISRAEL

Unfortunately, it is not only nations that have persecuted the Jewish people. The history of the Christian Church from its early years bears witness to a horrific catalogue of anti-Semitism through general insults, Church canons, ecclesiastical councils, imperial decrees and the false teaching of Replacement Theology, leading to the expulsion, persecution, torture, forced conversion, and murder of the Jews.

The average person, when asked, would deny that they were anti-Semitic. Yet many Christian believers in the UK and Europe have few, if any, thoughts or feelings about Israel. The reality is that for the majority of Christians, Israel has little or no significance in relation to their faith. This view is widespread, in spite of the fact that the Bible is a Jewish book and its central theme is God and Israel. Allowing for the fact that Luke may have been a Gentile, the Bible was written by about forty different Jewish men. The prophets are Jewish; they are first and foremost Israel's prophets. We Gentiles worship and serve a Jewish Saviour. After all, it is stated clearly in Scripture that salvation is first to the Jew and then to the Gentile (Romans 1:16). This is the fulfilment of God's promise that the whole world would be blessed through Abraham and his seed.

When writing to Gentile believers in Rome, Paul made it clear, for them and also for us, that God has not cast away His people (Romans 11:1). At this moment in time they are the 'branches ... broken off' (Romans 11:17), but if we believe the Word of God, the time is coming when they will be re-grafted into their own olive tree (Romans 11:24). Biblical teaching is clear, but the lack of understanding in the Church arises from a serious deficiency of biblical teaching in the body of Christ. The Church, and therefore individual believers, has been infected by an allegorical method of interpreting the Scriptures, which has prevailed from the second century onwards from the teaching of such men as Augustine, Chrysostom, Jerome, Ambrose of Milan and Origen.

Yes, all the blessings of Abraham are ours through faith in Christ (Galatians 3:14). But in including ourselves, we have excluded Israel to whom the promises were first given. Can it be right to rob Israel of its blessings and leave the Jewish people with the curses? This in itself is a failure to bless Israel and is a passive expression of anti-Semitism. Today, there is a new form or expression of anti-Semitism: anti-Israel or anti-Zionism. Christians who take such a position, whether or not they deny their belief in Replacement Theology, are fuelling Israel's enemies in their attempt to demonise and de-legitimise Israel and to rob the Jews of their land. Not only so, but they are in direct opposition to the God of the Bible. Anyone who reads the Bible cannot fail to notice that Zionism is a key theme; it is mentioned at least 161 times. Zion is not only the aspiration of the Jews but of God Himself.

'For the LORD has chosen Zion; He has desired it for His dwelling place'; 'For Zion's sake I will not hold My peace, And for Jerusalem's sake I will not rest,

Until her righteousness goes forth as brightness; And her salvation as a lamp that burns'; 'Yet I have set My King on My holy hill of Zion.'

(PSALM 132:13; ISAIAH 62:1; PSALM 2:6)

Let all those who hate Zion Be put to shame and turned back. Let them be as the grass on the housetops, Which withers before it grows up[.]

(PSALM 129:5,6)

The last part of the above verse ends in a curse. Careful reading indicates that those who are anti-Zion bring themselves under the power of this curse and will not flourish or prosper as a consequence, but will wither and die. Anti-Zionism can be described as a modern form of anti-Semitism. It seeks to deny the Jews their place in the land of Israel and to deny them the blessing that God has given to them. Much has been written about the nature and origins of anti-Semitism, but to my knowledge, very little has been written about the curse attached to anti-Semitism and its outworking in our personal and national life. Our treatment of the Jews determines whether God can bless us or whether He must curse us! This applies not only to an individual but to a nation as well. The pronouncement of God regarding blessing or cursing Abraham and his descendants recorded in Genesis 12 remain valid for all time (Genesis 12:1–3; 27:29; Numbers 24:9; Matthew 25:31–46).

THREE SOURCES OF CURSING

After many years of experience in healing and deliverance, I know that Christians can suffer from curses, which can be expressed through sickness, failure and an inability to experience God's love and power in all its fullness. Curses often come through the spoken word.

> Death and life are in the power of the tongue ...
>
> (PROVERBS 18:21)

Curses stem from three sources: God, Satan and human beings. Curses from Satan are usually communicated through witchcraft or Satanism. It is widely known that witches attempt to curse Christian marriages. A biblical example of curses from humans – although it is likely that Satan was behind this attempt through occult means, as he has access to willing human beings – is the attempt of Balak to curse the nation of Israel through Balaam (Numbers 22:4–6). We can curse our fellow human beings through speaking negatively; for example, 'I wish you had never been born.' Although this may start as a pronouncement, it can quickly become a curse in the life of the recipient. Remember, Jesus said that we are to:

> ... love your enemies, bless those who curse you, do good to those who hate you, and pray for those who spitefully use you and persecute you[.]
>
> (MATTHEW 5:44)

BLESSING OR CURSE
Before Moses died, he faced Israel with a stark choice:

> I call heaven and earth as witnesses today against you, that I have set before you life and death, blessing and cursing;

therefore choose life, that both you and your descendants may live[.]

(DEUTERONOMY 30:19)

I believe that disciples of Jesus today face the same choice; the condition for blessing or curse remains unchanged. For example, God's blessing on your sexuality is conditional. The only kind of sexual relationship that God can bless is the one that occurs between a man and a woman who are joined together in the covenant of marriage. Human beings cannot bless what God rejects, irrespective of the laws that governments pass to the contrary. There are spiritual and physical consequences for those who disobey God's ordinances. Sexual sin is one of the most common demonic entry points. For a better understanding of healing and deliverance, see *Healing through Deliverance* by Peter Horrobin.[75]

Whilst grace is unmerited favour, blessing is almost always the result of obedience. Disobedience and rebellion bring with them the possibility of discipline, sometimes experienced in the form of a curse. Contrary to the belief of many, followers of Jesus are not guaranteed unconditional protection from curses. Under the Law of Moses, the key to walking in God's blessing was to hear His voice and to obey Him (Deuteronomy 28:1). Under the New Covenant, the condition for blessing is the same; to hear the voice of the Lord and to obey Him (John 10:27). This can only be done as we abide in Jesus (John 14:21,23). However, if we fail to hear His voice or we deliberately disobey Him:

But it shall come to pass, if you do not obey the voice of the LORD your God, to observe carefully all His commandments

87

and His statutes which I command you today, that all these curses will come upon you and overtake you[.]

(DEUTERONOMY 28:15)

how shall we escape if we neglect so great a salvation, which at the first began to be spoken by the Lord, and wasconfirmed to us by those who heard Him, God also bearing witness both with signs and wonders, with various miracles, and gifts of the Holy Spirit, according to His own will[.] (Hebrews 2:3,4) Today, if you will hear His voice,

DO NOT HARDEN YOUR HEARTS. (HEBREWS 4:3)

Disobedience to God always has consequences. The book of James teaches us that when someone is tempted to do evil it is not God who tempts him, but they are drawn into sin by their own desires, and when sin is full grown it brings forth death (James 1:13–15). It seems that we have developed a sentimental view of God's love. We only have to consider God's judgements against Israel to see that such a view is not according to Scripture. The God who loves us is the one who will, when necessary, exercise strong discipline (Hebrews 12:5,6). God has the right to bless or curse. God's dealings with Israel are a model of His requirements for all people. The conditions for blessing and curse apply first to Israel and then to the nations. Jesus did not come to abolish God's moral and spiritual laws, but He did make provision for removing every curse when He died upon the cross (Matthew 5:17; Galatians 3:13).

THE NEW TESTAMENT AND GOD'S LAW

The teaching of the New Testament is clear: we are justified by faith and not by keeping the law (Romans 3:28). However, justification by faith does not invalidate the law. As the apostle Paul says:

> Do we then make void the law through faith? Certainly not! On the contrary, we establish the law.
>
> (ROMANS 3:31)

When asked by a lawyer, 'What is the greatest commandment?' Jesus replied by condensing the whole of the Ten Commandments into two: love God and love others (Matthew 22:37,38). In so doing, He was explaining the principle underlying the Ten Commandments: love expressed through faithfulness leads to obedience to God and responsibility for others expressed by a practical concern. To put it another way, how can we say we love the Lord and at the same time commit sin or injure our fellow human beings (John 14:21,23; Romans 6:1)? In John 14:21, Jesus refers to 'My commandments'. The commandments of the Son cannot be different to those of the Father, as the Son is the 'express image of His person' (Hebrews 1:3).

> Do not be deceived, God is not mocked; for whatever a man sows, that he will also reap. For he who sows to his flesh will of the flesh reap corruption, but he who sows to the Spirit will of the Spirit reap everlasting life.
>
> (GALATIANS 6:7,8)

THE GOD WHO BLESSES

Every good gift and every perfect gift is from above, and

comes down from the Father of lights, with whom there is no variation or shadow of turning.

(JAMES 1:17)

God's intention and desire is to bless His creation. The very first blessing bestowed upon humankind was the gift of life. Other created beings share that gift, but God gave humanity much more than life itself. He created male and female in His own image and after His own likeness. This is not so with other created beings such as the angels or the animals. This fact alone makes humankind absolutely unique in the whole of the created realms. It is no exaggeration to say that the creation of Adam and Eve is the crowning glory of creation. The angels radiate God's glory, but human beings express His image and likeness, and even in our fallen state this image, although spoiled through sin, can still be seen.

THE OUTWORKING OF BLESSING

The nature of blessing is expressed through 'fruitfulness':

God blessed them, and God said to them, 'Be fruitful and multiply; fill the earth and subdue it[.']

(GENESIS 1:28)

Here we see God blessing humankind's ability to produce after their own kind. God's blessings are communicated through covenant. Marriage is a covenant. A covenant differs from a contract in that a contract can be renegotiated or annulled, whereas a covenant cannot. Humans cannot expect to enjoy the covenant blessings of married life if they choose to ignore God's moral and spiritual values for the expression of their sexuality. When God blesses an individual, that person can be said to prosper and have success (Joshua 1:8).

FAITHFULNESS TO THE COVENANT RESULTS IN BLESSING

The following are some of the blessings that the Lord God promised to Israel if they were faithful in their worship to Him and if they refused to bow down to the gods of the nations:

> So you shall serve the LORD your God, and He will bless your bread and your water. And I will take sickness away from the midst of you. No one shall suffer miscarriage or be barren in your land; I will fulfill the number of your days. I will send My fear before you, I will cause confusion among all the people to whom you come, and will make all your enemies turn their backs to you.
>
> (EXODUS 23:25–27)

It is inconceivable that under the New Covenant God's blessings would be less than the above. Why is it, then, that so many believers today are sick and suffering from allergies that mean that they cannot eat certain foods? Infertility is widespread amongst men and women in the twenty-first century. Yet children are a blessings from the Lord. Surely, we cannot say that these believers are experiencing God's blessing on their food and water and reproductiveness.

THE CONSEQUENCE OF DISOBEDIENCE

The Law of Moses is described as the 'tutor to bring us to Christ' (Galatians 3:24). We cannot understand the need for the cross or the concept of blessing or curse unless we learn from the Law of Moses. The things that were written before (the whole of the Old Testament) were written to teach us (Romans 15:4).

The penalties for disobedience under the Law of Moses are best understood as the opposite of the blessings. If the people obeyed, God promised to bless everything they had (Deuteronomy 7:13–16). If they were unfaithful, He promised the exact reverse (Deuteronomy 28:15–68). We need to grasp that the God of the Old Testament is the God of the New Testament and that 'Jesus Christ is the same yesterday, today, and forever (Hebrews 13:8). Understanding this may lead to the root causes of many sicknesses which affect believers. No, I am not saying that we are under the Law of Moses, but that the consequences of sin in some cases may lead to sickness and the loss of God's blessing. Most Christians never look beyond repentance and forgiveness in dealing with the consequences of sin. It is clear from the Word of God that anti-Semitism is an offence against God Himself and therefore can lead to a loss of His blessing.

WHAT ARE THE CIRCUMSTANCES THAT CAUSE GOD TO CURSE?

As believers in Jesus we are not under the Law of Moses, but we are to obey the commands of Jesus. We need to acknowledge that there is both a temporal and eternal element to the Law of God. The Law of Moses is temporal. However, enshrined in the 613 commandments we shall discover spiritual principles valid for all time. It is precisely because God's law is rejected in this age that we have so many wars and so many injustices. Failure to honour one's parents, murder, adultery, stealing, bearing false witness and covetousness are still viewed by God as sin even though there is now forgiveness through the shed blood of Jesus. We can rest assured that the law of God will govern all nations during the millennial reign of Messiah:

> Many people shall come and say, 'Come, and let us go up to the mountain of the LORD, To the house of the God of Jacob; He will teach us His ways, And we shall walk in His paths.' For out of Zion shall go forth the law, And the word of the LORD from Jerusalem.
>
> (ISAIAH 2:3)

These penalties to Israel for unfaithfulness to the covenant came in the form of a curse (Deuteronomy 11:26–28; 28:58–68). A curse is an invisible spiritual power that robs the individual of God's blessing. Through disobedience we are robbed of God's blessing and opened up to the enemy's influence in our life (Ephesians 2:1 –3; Titus 3:3). The principle behind blessing or curse is the same under the New Covenant – obedience. Under the Mosaic Covenant, blessing was the result of obedience to the law. Under the New Covenant, blessing is the result of obedience to the Lord Jesus (John 10:27,28; 14:21,23).

We dare not deceive ourselves into thinking that we are protected from the curses if we are disobedient, for God is no respecter of persons and equal in His treatment of all humankind (Romans 11:19). The sins and their penalties outlined in Leviticus and Deuteronomy are an expression of God's standard for holiness: they detail His response to unfaithfulness, idolatry, immorality and rebellion. God never changes, so the expression of God's attitude to these sins is applicable for all time:

> God is not a man, that He should lie, Nor a son of man, that He should repent. Has He said, and will He not do? Or has He spoken, and will He not make it good?
>
> (NUMBERS 23:19)

'I will bless those who bless you, And I will curse him who curses you; And in you all the families of the earth shall be blessed' (Genesis 12:1–3). Those who mock, speak ill of or badly treat the Jewish people are guilty of cursing them. We should be in no doubt that any expression of anti-Semitism will result in God's curse.

Anti-Semitism undermines the believer's relationship and fellowship with the Lord by bringing them into direct opposition to the will of God. Those who teach that the Church has replaced Israel and that Israel has no future are in rebellion against the Word of God by denying His everlasting love for His ancient covenant people (Deuteronomy 7:7,8). God is being dishonoured, as He is being charged with unfaithfulness, turning away from His eternal promises, and lying (Numbers 23:9). In order to believe such teaching, words such as 'everlasting' are redefined to mean the exact opposite (Psalm 105:7–11).

THE CONSEQUENCES OF ANTI-SEMITISM
Anti-Semitism grieves and quenches the Holy Spirit in the life of the believer. The Holy Spirit is the Spirit of Truth (John 14:17; Ephesians 4:30; 1 Thessalonians 5:19). The

Holy Spirit is grieved when Christians speak ill of the Jewish people or when they promote false teaching such as Replacement Theology. Holding on to such wrong beliefs will inevitably lead to a loss of fellowship with the Lord and a separation from the presence of God and His power in our lives. Our service for the Lord will no longer have the fullness of His blessing.

Without the leading of the Holy Spirit, believers are left in the dark and in confusion. Those in this condition who seek an experience of God are open to spiritual deception. Christian leaders who are themselves deceived will lead others into the same deception. This is why teachers will be judged more strictly than other believers (James 3:1). There are many unclean spirits that seek to counterfeit the work of the Holy Spirit. 'And no wonder! For Satan himself transforms himself into an angel of light' (2 Corinthians 11:14). Deception makes a believer vulnerable to what the Bible calls 'the doctrines of demons' (1 Timothy 4:1; see Matthew 24:4; 2 Thessalonians 2:1–4).

Anti-Semitism undermines the believer's ability to distinguish between the work of counterfeiting demons and the work of the Holy Spirit (1 Corinthians 12:10). To allow deception into our lives concerning anti-Semitism is to open the door to further deception.

Anti-Semitism undermines the prayer life of the believer, as no longer can one say with a pure heart and mind: 'Hallowed by Your name. Your kingdom come. Your will be done On earth as it is in heaven' (Matthew 6:9,10). Why? Because when God's will and purposes for Israel have been rejected we are no longer praying for God's will to be done on earth in respect to the re-gathering of the Jewish people to the land of Israel and their subsequent acceptance of Jesus as Israel's Messiah (Ezekiel 36; Romans 11:26).

Anti-Semitism robs the believer of the full spiritual protection of the Lord and leaves the believer vulnerable to enemy attack. Ephesians 6:10–17 details the believers' spiritual protection. We are admonished to put on the full armour of God, which includes standing firm with the belt of truth buckled around the waist (v. 14). I believe that the truth protects us in the measure that we are willing to walk in it. The results of remaining in a condition of deception can lead to an inability to protect ourselves from demonic attack and can also lead to sickness and even death.

Anti-Semitism is more than likely to demonisation: individuals who allow anti-Semitism in their lives or who come from families characterised by anti-Semitism are likely to have given a foothold to the demonic in their lives, i.e. the spirit of antichrist (Ephesians 4:27). This can lead to sicknesses, depression and suicidal tendencies. In ministry we have seen that anti-Semitism can be the cause of sicknesses. On one occasion during a time of ministry, I encouraged those present to confess any anti-Semitism in their lives. The following day, one of the group testified she experienced an instant healing in her legs after she had done this. The only cure for this sin is repentance, renunciation, forgiveness and deliverance from demonic powers. Believers who join in protest with the BDS Campaign (Boycott, Divestment and Sanctions) to boycott Israeli goods, in order to turn opinion against Israel are, in fact, whether they are aware or not, joining themselves to the spirit of anti-Semitism.[76]

Please do not think that I am saying that Israel is above criticism; it is not. Currently, they are a secular state full of idolatry and immorality. However, the day will come when the Lord will cleanse them from their iniquities (Ezekiel 36:23–28).

THE CONSEQUENCES FOR THE CHURCH

Anti-Semitism robs the Church of the presence of the Lord. How can the Church expect to experience the manifest glory of His living presence when anti-Semitism, behind which is the spirit of antichrist, has not been repented of? To be anti-Semitic is to be anti-God. The word 'anti' in front of the word 'Christ' has two meanings. One means instead of, or another; it also means against. The spirit of antichrist is behind anti-Semitism as the agent of Satan who wishes to remove the Jewish people from the face of the earth. If he were able to do this, then unfulfilled prophecy relating to the second coming and Jesus' reign over the house of Jacob during the messianic period could not take place (Luke 1:32,33). Jesus will return to the Mount of Olives outside Jerusalem. There has to be a Jerusalem and there have to be Jews living in Israel (Acts 1:9–11; Zechariah 14:4). Anti-Semitism undermines the intention of God that the Church make the manifold wisdom of God known to the powers of darkness (Ephesians 3:10). Those who wrongly believe and teach that the Church has replaced Israel in the will and purposes of God are not proclaiming His truth in this matter (Romans 11:1,11).

Anti-Semitism opens the Church to the presence and power of the enemy through spirits of antichrist and deception leading to false practices in every area of Church life: worship, preaching, teaching, and the gifts of the Holy Spirit. The result will be a lack of unity leading to division within the body of Christ.

Anti-Semitism leads to a rejection of the Old Testament and, consequently, a loss of biblical understanding. The Pentateuchal curses are regarded as no longer relevant (Deuteronomy 28:15–68: Matthew 5:17). Rejection of the Jewish roots of Christianity leads to an erosion of the historic foundations of Christianity and unnecessarily separates Jew and Gentile. This was the sin of the 'German Christians', *die Deutsche Christen*, those Christians in Germany during the 1930s who embraced National Socialism (the Nazis: 1933–45) and welcomed Hitler as a 'messianic' leader. They ended up rejecting the whole of the Old Testament and those parts of the New Testament that were considered pro-Jewish. German theologians belonging to the 'German Christians' went as far as redefining Jesus as an Aryan. This is another example of a different gospel than the only true one. They denied that Jesus was a Jew because according to them, the New Testament portrays Jesus as being against the Jews. This, of course, is not true. However, Jesus did challenge corruption, hypocrisy and double standards (Matthew 7:5, 13:15, 21:12).

Anti-Semitism opens the way for the distortion of the true gospel. Jesus is a Jewish Messiah, and the preaching of any other Jesus allows a different spirit to operate and introduces another gospel than the one the apostle Paul preached (2 Corinthians 11:1–4). There are various contemporary distortions of the true gospel in the twenty-first century, such as the Dominion Theology and the Prosperity Gospel (Galatians 1:6).

Anti-Semitism leads to a loss of the New Testament ministry of Jesus in the area of miracles of healing and deliverance, and the authority and power required to defeat the powers of darkness and to destroy their works (John 14:12; 1 John 3:8b).

THE CONSEQUENCES OF ANTI-SEMITISM FOR A NATION

Anti-Semitism leads to confusion in politics and diplomacy. For example, in the Middle Eastern peace process, it seems that politicians are unable, or unwilling, to identify and deal with the real issue. So far, the Palestinian Arabs have turned down every United Nations resolution and every land compromise offered by Israel on the grounds that it would involve recognition of the State of Israel. Eight Arab heads of state met at an Arab summit in Khartoum on 1 September 1967, and agreed that there would be 'no peace with Israel, no recognition of Israel and no negotiations with Israel'.[77] If the Arabs will not recognise the state of Israel, what hope is there for peace? Why are world politicians failing to identify the main cause of the problems? How can there be peace when one side will not recognise the right of the other to exist, or to enter into negotiations?

It has to be said that Israel is in favour of the two state solution, although not willing for Jerusalem to be divided. In taking this position, the Israelis are willing to give away land that the Lord has said belongs to Him, and whose sovereignty is theirs, even though they are only tenants; they have no right to give it away (Leviticus 25:23). Although, they are understandably desperate for peace, God will not bless them in this.

In a recent speech at the UN General Assembly, September 26, 2013, President Mahmoud Abbas said, 'Let us envision another future... in which Israel will gain the recognition of 57 Arab and Muslim countries and where the States of Palestine and Israel will coexist in peace, in order to realize each people's hopes for progress and prosperity.'[78] In view of all that I have said so far, and at first glance, this seems like an amazing change of position by the Palestinians. However, this statement does not include recognition of Israel as a **Jewish** state. Shortly after President Abbas' statement, the Prime Minister of Israel, Benjamin Netanyahu, made it clear, in a speech on 7 October 2013 at Bar-Ilan University, that there must be recognition of Israel as a Jewish state, and that the Palestinians must give up the right of return for the 5 million Palestinians who are the sons, grandsons and in some case, the great grandsons of the original refugees from the 1948 War of Independence. Anti-Semitism has been described as the oldest and longest hatred in the world. If Israel were to comply with all the demands of the Palestinian Arabs, the question is, would it be enough to bring peace in the Middle East? The Palestinians have said no to peace with Israel on more than one occasion, even when they have been offered all the land they have demanded.

The United Nations and the EU, including the UK, are pursuing solutions that are aimed at dividing the land of Israel by agreeing to the establishment of east Jerusalem as a Palestinian capital. Those who attempt to interfere with Jerusalem are bringing their nation under the judgement of God.

I will also gather all nations, And bring them down to the Valley of Jehoshaphat; And I will enter into judgment with them there On account of My people, My heritage Israel,

Whom they have scattered among the nations; They have also divided up My land.

(JOEL 3:2)

And it shall happen in that day that I will make Jerusalem a very heavy stone for all peoples; all who would heave it away will surely be cut in pieces, though all nations of the earth are gathered against it.

(ZECHARIAH 12:3)

Anti-Semitism leads to a loss of national security: a nation's protection comes ultimately from God, and without His protection the nation has no complete means of guarding itself (Psalm 127:1). The security services cannot prevent every act of terrorism. A nation cannot ignore God and His laws and expect His protection (Psalm 147:13,14; Leviticus 26:6). 'Unless the LORD guards the city, The watchman stays awake in vain' (Psalm 127:1).

Anti-Semitism leads to the loss of national life and allows the foreigners to gain ascendancy: 'The alien who is among you shall rise higher and higher above you, and you shall come down lower and lower' (Deuteronomy 28:43). Whilst this applies in the first instance to Israel, it has application beyond Israel to other nations. The rise of Islam in many Western nations today has drastically changed Western life. For example, in the UK, forced marriages and Sharia law is practiced in Muslim communities.

Anti-Semitism leads to a loss of national identity, an often debated theme in many countries in the twenty-first century. For example, in Great Britain today there is much debate concerning the meaning and nature of citizenship. Britain is desperately seeking to discover its identity and to impart this identity to all new citizens. This is also the case for other nations such as Germany, Russia and Canada.

Anti-Semitism leads to a rise of self-interest that expresses itself through nationalism and political extremism. Extreme right-wing parties that are almost always anti-Semitic rise up against the foreigner in their midst. In the United Kingdom, the English Defence League is a modern example as is the British National Party.

Anti-Semitism is present in a number of different countries and political parties; for example, Russian political parties such as the Russian National Unity party, the Communist Party of the Russian Federation (KPRF, Russia's largest and best organised political organisation), and the Liberal Democratic Party of Russia (LDPR) led by the flamboyant ultranationalist Vladimir Zhirinovsky. Russian politicians who are known for their anti-Semitic statements have been re-elected to the parliament; for example, A. Makashov and N. Kondratenko.

In the Ukraine, Jews have risen to prominent, visible positions, such as the mayors of Odessa and Vinnitsa. Nevertheless, despite higher visibility and improved statements from national leaders, anti-Semitism continues on the local level. Ultra nationalist Ukrainian groups such as UNSO and DSU circulate anti-Semitic tracts, and anti-Semitic articles appear regularly in some local newspapers, particularly in Western Ukraine and Kiev.

Anti-Semitism leads to an increase of Jewish persecution and attacks against the Jewish community. This consequence for the Jewish population is that they become the scapegoat of society's ills; they suffer personal attacks, property attacks and graveyard desecration.

Anti-Semitism, which became a central policy of the Nazi government, meant that the murder of Jews was the outworking of government policy. In order for this policy to be carried, it required the cooperation of the judiciary, the professions – such as civil servants and teachers – and even the Church, although the main guilt here was silence. The law became a tool for evil. Something similar will happen before the coming of Jesus, only this time it will not be just one nation that follows an evil government and its wicked policies, but the whole world.

In the days yet to come, when the antichrist governs – he is sometimes referred to as 'the son of perdition' (2 Thessalonians 2: 3,4), or 'the lawless one' (v. 8). Revelation 13 describes him as a beast that came out of the sea. There will be one world government. The antichrist will rule the world. '... authority was given him over every tribe, tongue, and nation ...' (Revelation 13:7,8). Those whose names are not written in the book of life will worship the beast, the whole world will worship the beast, '... and they worshiped the beast, saying, 'Who is like the beast? Who is able to make war with him?' (Revelation 13:4).

This man who opposes God will be given authority for a short time, forty-two months (Revelation 13:5). And he will 'make war with the saints' (Revelation 13:7). Then when Jesus comes, he will be captured along with the false prophet and 'cast alive into the lake of fire' (Revelation 19:20).

Anti-Semitism in a nation leads to conflicting ideologies standing together as they attack Israel. For example, socialists and Islamists.[79] Most Western nations refuse to see the real intention of Islam in their midst. For evidence of this point see *Eurabia: The Euro-Arab Axis* by Bat Ye'or.[80] Whenever there is a terrorist action they are quick to distinguish radical Islam from peace-loving Islam. Islam was founded and spread by the sword. This leads governments to appease the Muslim community. The UK government seems to overlook the use of Sharia law amongst Muslims to settle their disputes.[81] Multiculturalism is not working and reinforces the fact that people are living in a divided society. We should welcome the foreigner in our midst if they are willing to abide by our laws. If not, then the home nation will be eventually supplanted and will become the tail and not the head.

Anti-Semitism leads to a weak economy: God cannot bless the finances of a nation that allows anti-Semitism in its home or foreign policy. A nation without God's blessing on its finances will get into serious debt and become dependent upon foreign investment (Deuteronomy 28:44). As I write this, Western nations are in serious financial decline. Apparently some two-thirds of the 192 nations that comprise the United Nations are in agreement with the establishment of a Palestinian state with east Jerusalem as its capital. If this becomes a reality, the intention of the Palestinian Arabs is to forbid Jews from accessing the 'Kotel', the Western Wall. In fact they would be forbidden from entering any part of east Jerusalem. Furthermore, these countries wish to drive Israel back to the 1967 borderlines. These are not borderlines agreed between two nations seeking peace with one another. They are the 1949 armistice lines where the fighting stopped, and they are indefensible, making it impossible for Israel to protect itself against military attack. For further information on these so-called borders see the article by Alan Baker, 'The Fallacy of the "1967 Borders" – No Such Borders Ever Existed'.[82]

Anti-Semitism leads to a lack of scientific integrity: human life is seen by many as a product of time and chance, where life has no real meaning and value. Consequently, abortion is seen as acceptable. In this light, euthanasia is seen as a mercy, equivalent to putting an animal out of its misery by ending its life. This view has opened the way for abortion, which is nothing less than the murder of unborn babies, the equivalent to the sacrifice of babies to the demon Molech, which was a practice of the nations surrounding Israel; a practice forbidden to Israel (Leviticus 18:21). Sadly, Israel sinned in this respect, and King Solomon built high places for the worship of Molech (1 Kings 11:7). The demon god Molech still lives and is still worshipped today through the nations' health services.

The spirit of humanism rules in today's world. Young women are encouraged to exercise their right to abortion at the expense of their unborn child's right to life. They are told that it is a small thing and they will soon get over it. This is not so; the author has experience in seeking to bring the healing of Jesus into the lives of women who have had abortions, who are tormented by emotional and physical problems such as mental illness, guilt and condemnation.

Present legislation in several Western nations allows experimentation on live embryos. Where will scientific research take us, unless God steps in? The world has not learned from the history of the Nazi death camps and their 'scientists' whose research interests led to cruel and wicked experiments upon living human beings. The relevant question here is: When does human life begin – at conception or at birth (Psalm 139:13–16; Zechariah 12:1b)?

Anti-Semitism leads to the demise of Christian religion:

anti-Semitism strengthens the presence of religions that hold and preach a doctrine of *Judenhass*, hatred of the Jew.

Pastor Niemöller was a Lutheran pastor during the Second World War. At the end of the war, he made the following comment:

> They came first for the Communists, and I didn't speak up because I wasn't a Communist. Then they came for the Jews, and I didn't speak up because I wasn't a Jew. Then they came for the trade unionists, and I didn't speak up because I wasn't a trade unionist. Then they came for the Catholics, and I didn't speak up because I was a Protestant. Then they came for me, and by that time no one was left to speak up.[83]

"Saturday kill Jews, Sunday kill Christians", is the claim of the Islamists.[84] Christians are clearly in the sights of militant Islam, by such terrorist groups as Boko Haram, and al-Shabab, which is linked to al-Qaeda. The recent Westgate Shopping Mal attack in Nairobi is an example. It was clearly non-Muslims who were the target of the terrorist gunmen.[85] The terrorists were asking shoppers questions regarding the Quran, if answered correctly, or if they declared that they were Muslims, they were allowed to leave the Mal, if not they were shot.[86] It is a fact that Christians are currently persecuted, tortured and killed in Muslim countries such as Egypt, Syria, Nigeria, Sudan, and Pakistan.

It is now time for Christian believers to stand up for Israel! Are we going to repeat the sins of our fathers, most of who said nothing in protest as the Jews were being slaughtered and sent to concentration camps? Is it not time for us to demonstrate Christ's love for them to make them jealous for the Jesus who lives in us (Romans 11:11)? Is it not time for us to unconditionally love our elder brother? If not, how are we going to face Jesus when we meet Him?

> Then He will also say to those on the left hand, 'Depart from Me, you cursed, into the everlasting fire prepared for the devil and his angels: for I was hungry and you gave Me no food; I was thirsty and you gave Me no drink; I was a stranger and you did not take Me in, naked and you did not clothe Me, sick and in prison and you did not visit Me.' Then they also will answer Him, saying, 'Lord, when did we see You hungry or thirsty or a stranger or naked or sick or in prison, and did not minister to You?' Then He will answer them, saying, 'Assuredly, I say to you, inasmuch as you did not do it to one of the least of these, you did not do it to Me.' And these will go away into everlasting punishment, but the righteous into eternal life.
>
> (MATTHEW 25:41–46)

CHAPTER 4

HOW TO CLEANSE THE LAND FROM BLOODGUILT

The purpose of this chapter is to provide guidelines for praying at sites where Jewish blood has been shed, to ask the Lord to lift His curse. There are many such sites, especially in Europe. For example, 1.5 million Jews were murdered on Ukrainian soil during the Second World War between the years 1941–45. In Smolensk, Russia, like the Ukraine, many Jewish people were summarily executed, gassed or burnt to death. What we discovered in Smolensk is that these sites are cursed by God. This curse hangs over the surrounding area: the village, the town, the community, and the church, affecting spiritual life and growth and the preaching of the gospel. This should not surprise us, as the ground that has received the shed blood cries out to God.

> And He said, 'What have you done? The voice of your brother's blood cries out to Me from the ground.'
>
> (GENESIS 4:10)

THE HISTORY OF JEWISH SUFFERING

'... The earth will also disclose her blood, And will no more cover her slain' (Isaiah 26:21). The scripture is clear that the day is coming when God will judge those guilty of murder, as their deeds will be exposed to the light of God's judgement. How loud is the cry that reaches God from all the Jewish bloodshed in the history of the nations? There is hardly a country where Jews have not been rejected, persecuted, tortured and killed. I believe that the attitude of indifference exhibited by many Christians would change dramatically if they were to consider the history of the Jewish people. The history of Jewish persecution and suffering that is indelibly written on every Jewish heart is largely unknown to the average Christian.

ASHAMED TO BE A CHRISTIAN?

When I began to investigate the history of Jewish persecution by the Church, I was appalled. I found it hard to understand how people could call themselves Christian and yet act so contrary to the teaching of Jesus. It became apparent to me that the Jewish people must struggle to overcome a natural fear and horror when the name of Christ is mentioned. Would it shock you if I said that as far as Jewish people are concerned, the Holocaust was perpetrated by baptised Christians – Roman Catholic and Protestant?

Yes, the world stood by whilst Germany, a 'Christian nation', a nation blessed by having the Bible translated into the German language and a state Church, annihilated the Jews. The one who accomplished this remarkable achievement of translation was a national hero to the Nazis, Martin Luther, the great reformer and author of the modern

German language. Yet sadly, as we have seen, in his latter days he became an anti-Semite.

THE SIN OF THE NATIONS

Germany is not alone in such behaviour. Edward I evicted the Jews from England in 1290.[87] Not only so, but Jews were massacred at Clifford's Tower in York in 1190.[88] It is interesting to note that it was under Oliver Cromwell that the Jews were readmitted to England.[89] Jews were expelled from Spain in 1492.[90]

Germany has done much to acknowledge and deal with its gruesome past.[91] Currently, the German education system includes teaching on the nation's Nazi past, and Holocaust studies.[92] There are several Christian ministries in Germany who love and bless the Jewish people and care for Holocaust survivors. However, nationally, there is a difference between Germany and England in respect to our anti-Semitic past. Germany is conscious of its guilt; Britain is not. It is not hard to see how evil treatment of Jewish people could be justified and carried out by Christians when we understand the pernicious influence of anti-Semitism stemming from the teaching and preaching in the early Church. The joining of state and Church, the altar and the crown, reinforced this anti-Semitism, following the declaration of Christianity as the official religion of the Roman Empire by Constantine the Great.

HOW DOES THEIR SIN AFFECT US?

By now, you may be asking a significant question: what has all this to do with me? Surely it's all in the past? Although we are not directly responsible for the sins of others and for the sins of our ancestors, we do have a responsibility to separate ourselves from their sins. We are called to confess and renounce their sins as well as to forgive them for the consequences of their sins as they affect us today.

Let us begin by looking at what the Bible says concerning the need to confess the sins of our ancestors.

> But if they confess their iniquity and the iniquity of their fathers, with their unfaithfulness in which they were unfaithful to Me, and that they also have walked contrary to Me, and that I also have walked contrary to them and have brought them into the land of their enemies; if their uncircumcised hearts are humbled, and they accept their guilt – then I will remember My covenant with Jacob, and My covenant with Isaac and My covenant with Abraham I will remember; I will remember the land.
>
> (LEVITICUS 26:40–42)

This scripture is addressed to the Israelites and comes in the chapter where God is laying down the conditions for blessing or curse. God warns the Israelites what the consequences of unfaithfulness to the covenant will bring. Their enemies will pursue them and God will evict them from the land and scatter them among the nations where they will perish.

> You shall perish among the nations, and the land of your enemies shall eat you up. And those of you who are left shall waste away in their iniquity in your enemies' lands; also **in their fathers' iniquities**, which are with them, they shall waste away.
>
> (LEVITICUS 26: 38,39)

Notice the words that I have highlighted: the iniquity of their fathers. It is not just the sins of the present generation that God takes into account, but also the sins of those who have gone before. There is no such thing as private sin; our sin always affects others, even those not yet born. For example, the whole of the human race has been affected by the sin of Adam (Romans 5:12). This is because there is a spiritual link between him and us. This spiritual link also exists between us and our more immediate ancestors (Exodus 20:5; Jeremiah 32:18; Lamentations 5:7). Forgiving our ancestors for their sins does not mean that as a consequence of our prayer they themselves are forgiven, but only that we are agreeing with God's verdict that their actions were sinful. We are not condemning or judging them, but forgiving them, as the consequences of their sins have been visited upon us.

The whole of the human race has been affected by the sin of Adam (Romans 5:12). This is because there is a spiritual connection between Adam and all his descendants. The scripture is clear; it was through Adam that sin and death entered the world, bringing death to humankind, the animals, and the whole of creation. In confessing the sins of our ancestors we are separating ourselves –cutting ourselves off – from their sins in order that we may be freed from the consequences, through the application of the shed blood of Christ who has freed us from all the consequences of sin (Galatians 3:13).

GOD'S REQUIREMENT FOR THE RESTORATION OF HIS BLESSING
In Leviticus 26, we find not just a warning regarding the

consequences of sin, but God's remedy when sin occurs. The action God calls for is two-fold: first, we need to confess our own sins and to repent of any personal anti-Semitism. We are personally responsible for acknowledging, confessing and repenting of our own sin. The second requirement for God to bring healing and restoration is to confess the sins of our ancestors. The word 'confession' means to agree with God's verdict on our sin. When we confess our sins, we are not telling God something that He doesn't know. We are agreeing with God that we have sinned. In confessing the sins of our ancestors, we are not declaring personal guilt but agreeing with God that they have sinned. We are declaring that we will not sin as they did. Each generation must distance itself from the sins of the previous generation. We must not bow down to the idols of our ancestors. A biblical example of this is Gideon:

> Now it came to pass the same night that the LORD said to him, 'Take your father's young bull, the second bull of seven years old, and tear down the altar of Baal that your father has, and cut down the wooden image that is beside it; and build an altar to the LORD your God on top of this rock in the proper arrangement, and take the second bull and offer a burnt sacrifice with the wood of the image which you shall cut down.'
>
> (JUDGES 6:25,26)

Each generation is faced with a choice: we either serve the gods of our ancestors or we worship the Lord. Joshua declared: 'But as for me and my house, we will serve the LORD' (Joshua 24:15). We do not have to bear the consequences of the sins of our ancestors (Exodus 20:5). The consequences of their sin could be that we are carrying their guilt or that we are failing to experience the fullness of God's blessings because a curse has been visited upon us. The scripture is clear: 'Christ has redeemed us from the curse of the law, having become a curse for us' (Galatians 3:13). The Lord Jesus has shed His blood: that is more than sufficient to deal with any sin. However, although His blood has been shed, it is only effective when it is applied to the specific sin. Remember the Passover? Once the blood of the lamb had been shed it was to be applied to the two doorposts and to the lintel of the house (Exodus 12:6,7). It provided protection from the angel of death after it had been applied.

We see such confession of the sins of the ancestors in two great prayers in the Bible, one by Nehemiah and the other by Daniel.

> please let Your ear be attentive and Your eyes open, that You may hear the prayer of Your servant which I pray before You now, day and night, for the children of Israel Your servants, and confess the sins of the children of Israel which we have sinned against You. Both my father's house and I have sinned.
>
> (NEHEMIAH 1:6)

Nehemiah not only confesses his own sin ('and I have sinned') but he confesses the sins of his father's house ('Both my father's house and I have sinned.') Daniel's prayer also has much to teach us about confessing the sins of the nation.

> O LORD, righteousness belongs to You, but to us shame of face, as it is this day – to the men of Judah, to the inhabitants of Jerusalem and all Israel, those near and those far off in

all the countries to which You have driven them, because of the unfaithfulness which they have committed against You. O Lord, to us belongs shame of face, to our kings, our princes, and our fathers, because we have sinned against You.

(DANIEL 9:7,8)

Daniel confesses the sins of others: those who had gone before, fathers, even rulers, kings and princes. Some wrongly call this 'identificational repentance'. If these actions of Nehemiah and Daniel are to be described beyond the simple word 'confession', I believe a much more biblical term is 'identificational confession'. 'Repentance' is a word that the Bible reserves for personal sin from which an individual is commanded to turn away. See Ezekiel 14:6:

Therefore say to the house of Israel, thus says the Lord GOD: 'Repent, turn away from your idols, and turn your faces away from all your abominations.'

Similarly, Paul admonishes the people to 'repent, turn to God, and do works befitting repentance' (Acts 26:20).

RENOUNCING THE SINS OF OUR ANCESTORS

Repentance and confession deal with the past, and renunciation and consecration – a fresh commitment to the Lord – deal with the future. When I renounce sin, I am saying that this sin will have no part of my life from this moment on and in the future. It is equivalent to Joshua saying:

And if it seems evil to you to serve the LORD, choose for yourselves this day whom you will serve, whether the gods which your fathers served that were on the other side of the River, or the gods of the Amorites, in whose land you dwell. But as for me and my house, we will serve the LORD.'

(JOSHUA 24:15)

FORGIVING THE SINS OF OUR ANCESTORS

Now we come to another important action, that of forgiveness. Because the sins of our ancestors have visited iniquity upon us and affected us spiritually, we need to deal with them. Forgiving the sins of others deals with the spiritual consequences of their sins which, although committed in the past, still have power over us. Forgiveness separates us from those who committed specific sins and enables us to break the power or effect of the sin, so that we can deal with its present-day consequences. Jesus taught us to forgive the sins of others, 'For if you forgive men their trespasses, your heavenly Father will also forgive you. But if you do not forgive men their trespasses, neither will your Father forgive your trespasses' (Matthew 6:14,15); 'bless those who curse you, and pray for those who spitefully use you' (Luke 6:28).

When the consequence of the sins of our ancestors has been to open us up to cursing, then we need to forgive them. This forgiveness does not just apply to those who are alive, as we are also living with the consequences of the sins of our ancestors. This can be seen in the curse arising from the shedding of Jewish blood.

SUMMARY

RENUNCIATION

To renounce sin and Satan is to declare that we wish no part with them. This action affects the future. It is a declaration that we will not sin in this way again and that this sin no longer has any power over or through us.

CONFESSING AND FORGIVING

This deals with the past. Forgiving our ancestors for their sins does not mean that as a consequence of our prayer they themselves are forgiven, but only that we are agreeing with God's verdict that their actions were sinful. Neither are we condemning them but forgiving them, as the consequences of their sins have been visited upon us.

DEFILEMENT THROUGH THE SHEDDING OF INNOCENT BLOOD

The Law of Moses teaches that human life is sacred and states that the penalty for murder is death. Although the death penalty has been abolished in most Western nations, it is important to understand that God required the death of the murderer. This was the only way that the defilement of shed blood could be cleansed.

> Whoever kills a person, the murderer shall be put to death on the testimony of witnesses; but one witness is not sufficient testimony against a person for the death penalty. Moreover you shall take no ransom for the life of a murderer who is guilty of death, but he shall surely be put to death. ... So you shall not pollute the land where you are; for blood defiles the land, and no atonement can be made for the land, for the blood that is shed on it, except by the blood of him who shed it.
>
> (NUMBERS 35:30,31,33)

The shedding of blood as a deliberate act of murder pollutes or defiles the land. Anyone guilty of manslaughter – that

118

is, who killed another accidentally – could flee to a city of refuge where he had to stay until the high priest died. Only then could he return to his own home (Numbers 35:9–29). If he ventured outside the city of refuge, the avenger of blood could kill him. It was the ancient custom that a member of the victim's family had the right to avenge the death by shedding the blood of the murderer.

The basis for the death penalty of the murderer had been established in the days of Noah. As Noah came out of the ark and before the human race repopulated itself, God informed Noah that human life was sacred and that He would demand a reckoning from everyone who murdered another, life for life (Genesis 9:6). Presumably prior to this, as violence had spread across the earth, there had been no penalty to discourage the act of murder (Genesis 6:11).

Let us ask a significant question: why would blood soaked up by the ground cause the land to become defiled or polluted? In *Reclaiming the Ground*, I described how land can become defiled through human sin, because it gives access to unclean spirits. As there is nothing essentially unclean about human blood, an organic substance, then we won't be surprised to find a similar answer. In order to better understand this we need to turn to Numbers 19 which deals with the laws of purification following death where someone has had contact with a dead body.

> He who touches the dead body of anyone shall be unclean seven days. He shall purify himself with the water on the third day and on the seventh day; then he will be clean. But if he does not purify himself on the third day and on the seventh day, he will not be clean. Whoever touches the body of anyone who

has died, and does not purify himself, defiles the tabernacle of the LORD. That person shall be cut off from Israel. He shall be unclean, because the water of purification was not sprinkled on him; his uncleanness is still on him. This is the law when a man dies in a tent: All who come into the tent and all who are in the tent shall be unclean seven days; and every open vessel, which has no cover fastened on it, is unclean. Whoever in the open field touches one who is slain by a sword or who has died, or a bone of a man, or a grave, shall be unclean seven days. And for an unclean person they shall take some of the ashes of the heifer burnt for purification from sin, and running water shall be put on them in a vessel. A clean person shall take hyssop and dip it in the water, sprinkle it on the tent, on all the vessels, on the persons who were there, or on the one who touched a bone, the slain, the dead, or a grave. The clean person shall sprinkle the unclean on the third day and on the seventh day; and on the seventh day he shall purify himself, wash his clothes, and bathe in water; and at evening he shall be clean. But the man who is unclean and does not purify himself, that person shall be cut off from among the assembly, because he has defiled the sanctuary of the LORD. The water of purification has not been sprinkled on him; he is unclean. It shall be a perpetual statute for them. He who sprinkles the water of purification shall wash his clothes; and he who touches the water of purification shall be unclean until evening. Whatever the unclean person touches shall be unclean; and the person who touches it shall be unclean until evening.

(NUMBERS 19:11–22)

Why does contact with a dead body make a person unclean and require ritual cleansing? Perhaps you are already thinking that disease can be present in someone who dies? Well this may be a factor; for example, when someone dies in a tent (v. 14) every open vessel without a cover presents the danger of spreading infection from someone who has died from an infectious disease. What about someone who has been killed by a sword? In such circumstances death occurs from blood loss and trauma. If burial does not occur quickly after death, then it is possible that there is a danger of infection. It is normal practice in the Middle East for burial to take place on the day of death. What about touching a person's bone or even a grave? Is there still a danger of infection? Some people die because they stop breathing, their heart fails or they experience a severe stroke. In these circumstances there is normally no presence of infection. Nevertheless, 'Whoever touches the dead body of anyone who has died, and does not purify himself, defiles the tabernacle of the LORD.'

This defilement arises as a consequence of touching the dead because evil spirits can be present. As disciples of Jesus, we can ask for His protection. Evil spirits can be present either because the person was murdered, or they have gained a foothold in the dead person during their lifetime (Ephesians 4:27). Sin provides an open door for evil spirits; they are unclean and cause defilement. Evil spirits are present in the history of Israel and in the history of the Church. The worship of idols leads to demonisation.

> They provoked Him to jealousy with foreign gods; With abominations they provoked Him to anger. They sacrificed to demons, not to God, To gods they did not know, To new gods ...
>
> (DEUTERONOMY 32:16,17)

They even sacrificed their sons And their daughters to
demons, And shed innocent blood, The blood of their sons
and daughters, Whom they sacrificed to the idols of Canaan;
And the land was polluted with blood. Thus they were defiled
by their own works ...

(PSALM 106:37–39)

One of the consequences of Adam's sin was the loss of his
dominion over the world (Genesis 1:26). It was at this time
that Satan became the ruler or the prince of this world (Luke
4:5,6; 1 John 5:19; John 14:30). From the sin of Adam, Satan
and the powers of darkness have tormented and tempted
human beings into sin, in order that they may gain access to
their lives. There is no record in the Old Testament of anyone
taking authority over evil spirits and casting them out. By the
time of Jesus, there were Jewish exorcists, but clearly, they
had no authority or power (Acts 19:13–17). Freedom from
tormenting spirits and cleansing from their defilement under
the Mosaic Law was different before the incarnation of Jesus.
For example, when King Saul was tormented by an evil spirit,
David had to play his harp in worship of the Lord before the
spirit would depart (1 Samuel 16:14,23).

It was human rebellion that gave Satan the right of entry
into this world. Before Satan sinned, heaven, and not earth,
was his place of habitation. When Adam sinned, he was
separated from the source of his dominion authority – God.
Jesus was the first man after Adam (before Adam's fall) to
be without sin. When Jesus was born, He was not under
the law because He had no sin. When Jesus began verbally
commanding evil spirits to come out, people were astonished;
they were amazed at His authority (Mark 1:21– 28). The

good news is that Jesus has delegated to His disciples the authority to cast out evil spirits (Matthew 10:1; Luke 10:17).

What happens to evil spirits when the person they are living in dies? The answer is that they look for another home. The transference of evil spirits at death to one who is present or one who touches the dead body is well known by those with experience in healing and deliverance. Under the Mosaic Law, freedom from contact with the dead and the subsequent defilement from evil spirits came for the individual through the prescribed ritual, such as the sprinkling of a person with the water of purification, in which were the ashes of a red heifer (Numbers 19:13). It is clear that the Lord would not allow unclean spirits into the community of God's people or into His holy tabernacle, so He provided deliverance through the water of cleansing. So, now we have our answer to what caused the ground to be defiled or polluted when it received the blood of the murdered victim; unclean spirits were given access through the murder. Before Jesus shed His blood on the cross, murder could only be atoned for, or covered by, the death of the murderer.

An example of the consequences of bloodguilt can be found in the case of Saul and the Gibeonites. The famine in the days of David was caused by Saul's guilt in murdering the Gibeonites. By this time Saul was dead. The bloodguilt of the Gibeonites was visited upon his descendants and was removed only when seven descendants of Saul were put to death (2 Samuel 21:1,6,9,14). Under certain circumstances – such as when the murderer could not be found – bloodguilt could be removed through animal sacrifice (Deuteronomy 21). Places that have been defiled can be made holy again (2 Chronicles 29:3–17). I believe that we can say that following the death of Jesus for the sins of the world, we may apply the atonement of His shed blood to any defilement that we come across.

THE SHEDDING OF JEWISH BLOOD

When we consider the murder of Jewish people, we find that we are facing something more than the presence of unclean spirits. We are looking at a curse that has been placed by the living God because the blood shed is from one of Abraham's descendants. When God said that He would curse those who cursed Abraham and his descendants, He meant it. Now there are three sources of cursing that we need to consider: satanic curses, human curses and curses from God.

SATAN'S ATTEMPT TO CURSE ISRAEL

Satan continually seeks opportunities to curse humankind, especially the people of God, through witchcraft or Satanism. Occult means of cursing have been used for years. One example is when Balak wanted to curse the children of Israel. At the request of Balak, Balaam tried three times to curse the people of Israel (Numbers 22:10,11). He discovered that it is against the will of God to curse those whom God has chosen to bless (Numbers 22:12), so he was forced into blessing them. It is my belief that Satan was behind this attempt to curse the Israelites.

However, when Satan is unsuccessful in bringing his curses, he uses another strategy. If he can provoke God's people into disobedience, they will automatically come under the penalty of breaking the covenant. Sometime later, Israel committed idolatry by joining in the worship of Baal of Peor, the god of the Moabites (Numbers 25). This was at the advice of

Balaam (Numbers 31:16). The consequence of their idolatry and sexual immorality was God's judgement: 24,000 died of a plague sent by God, and the leaders were put to death.

HUMAN BEINGS CAN CURSE ONE ANOTHER

We can use our tongue to curse our fellow believers (1 Kings 2:8; James 3:6–9). The power of life and death is in the tongue (Proverbs 18:21). I can testify to receiving healing through deliverance from a severe case of vertigo caused by spirits of infirmity that had been given rights from the negative words of fellow believers! This occurred following rejection from fellow leaders when I attempted to introduce the healing and deliverance ministry into the local church. Jesus warned us not to curse others but instead to bless them (Matthew 5:44; Luke 6:28; Romans 12:14). Sometimes people curse themselves with their own words (Genesis 27:13; Matthew 27:25).

The way to deal with curses from Satan sent from those involved in witchcraft or Satanism is to forgive the one who did the cursing. These curses normally come via some form of ritual taking place in a coven. Witchcraft is practised all over the world. Since the repeal of the Witchcraft Act in the UK, which occurred on 22 June in 1951,[93] witches may now practise their craft without fear of prosecution. For example, it is well known among those with experience in healing and deliverance to those involved in witchcraft that witches target Church leaders and their families, and seek through cursing to bring about sickness and to destroy Christian marriages. They also seek to disrupt Christian meetings.[94]

An Anglican vicar from a parish in Lancashire, a friend of the author, was one day visited by a woman who knocked at his door and asked for information about becoming a

Christian. He showed her into his study and then went to make her a cup of tea. When he returned, they began a conversation that was suddenly interrupted by the woman who, somewhat startled, made a comment along the lines of the words, 'I know that your God is more powerful than mine.' She had visited the vicar with the hope of cursing him with sickness, by bringing an object that had been prayed over in the coven. When placing the object on his study table, she had unknowingly placed it upon a Bible. The woman was frightened when suddenly the object was thrown to the floor!

As '... a curse without cause shall not alight ...' (Proverbs 26:2). Sin makes us vulnerable to such curses, so we may need to confess personal sin which has been the entry point for the curse to land upon us. It is only through seeking the Lord for His confirmation that we can know if we have been cursed in this way.

Baptism in the Holy Spirit is a vital prerequisite for the most effective Christian service. We need to be constantly filled with the Holy Spirit (Ephesians 5:18). We need the Holy Spirit to come upon us if we are to receive the necessary power for Christian ministry (Acts 1:8). Without the 'Promise of the Father' (Acts 1:4), we cannot access all the gifts of the Spirit needed to proclaim the kingdom of God (Acts 1:8). Without the gift of being able to distinguish between spirits, we may be open to confusion (1 Corinthians 12:10). When we have been cursed via coven activity, we obviously do not know the person or persons involved. However, in this case we do not need to know who cursed us, but we do need to forgive them. Then we can take authority over the curse and break its power over us. It is a similar procedure when another human being curses us.

GOD CAN CURSE THOSE WHO OPPOSE HIS WILL
(Genesis 12:1–3; Deuteronomy 11:26–28; 30:19)

Abraham and his descendants, the Jewish people, are so important to God in His plan to bless all the other nations that God pronounces both a blessing and a curse surrounding the treatment of this special people. The direct consequence of cursing the Jewish people is to bring the individual or a nation under a curse directly from God Himself. Of all the curses, this one is the most powerful (Isaiah 60:12).

However, when it comes to a curse applied by God Himself, we cannot deal with it in the usual way, as we do not have authority over God! Jesus has given to us His authority over Satan (Luke 10:18–20), but clearly our authority is limited when it comes to God. In this case, we need to ask God to remove His curse.

SEEKING GOD FOR THE REMOVAL OF HIS CURSE
All that we have learned so far are the first steps: confession, renunciation and forgiveness. I will provide a model prayer, not to be followed exactly, but to demonstrate the essential principles.

NEW COVENANT PROCEDURE FOR CLEANSING FROM THE SHEDDING OF JEWISH BLOOD
According to the Law of Moses, it was necessary to bring an animal sacrifice in order to be forgiven. It was the only way that sin could be covered and the land cleansed from defilement, for without the shedding of blood there was no forgiveness of sin (Hebrews 9:22). Since Jesus has shed His blood, this is now the basis for all forgiveness and cleansing (Colossians 1:14; 1 John 1:9).

We must confess any personal sin before confessing the sins of our ancestors, especially if we have been guilty of the sin of anti-Semitism. We need to forgive our own nation – its government and institutions – for their bad treatment of Jewish people and for unjust laws that have been passed that have penalised the Jewish community. We need to confess the sins of Christians against the Jewish people, including the Church and our own particular denomination.

Jesus taught us to forgive others who sin against us (Matthew 6:14). The point here is that the sins our ancestors have committed have a direct effect on us. This is certainly true of Adam's sin (Romans 5:13). Consider the sin that led to the Babylon captivity. During the seventy years of their exile, many Jews were born into the captivity caused by their parents' sin.

CLEANSING PRAYERS FROM THE SHEDDING OF JEWISH BLOOD

The following prayers are to be viewed as guidelines. It is not intended that they be followed slavishly; they need adapting to local conditions, and the leading of the Holy Spirit is essential. They contain spiritual concepts and are provided to suggest an approach to these issues. They are not according to the laws of the Medes and Persians.

A representative of the nation that committed the crime needs to be present. So, if the murder occurred during the Second World War and the victims were Jewish, it requires a German or Russian citizen. A pastor or town official who is a believer is ideal. Prayer action requires a lot of preparation beforehand in order to discover the exact nature of the evil deed and those responsible. It needs someone to take the lead, as well as full understanding and agreement amongst those present for the prayer action. This requires good communication between participants and the prior circulation of information. The leader can first offer a general prayer declaring the reason for the prayer action, what occurred in this place, and when it happened. Then he can ask the Lord to cleanse the place. After this, representatives of the nations that carried out the murder can come forward and pray. The following prayers are context sensitive and some of them will need to be adapted to each particular prayer action. It is advisable to begin by proclaiming that Jesus is Lord.

LORDSHIP PRAYER
We declare before God and the whole company of heaven and earth that today we submit ourselves to the Lordship of Jesus over His Church in this town (name specific churches). It is our intention to hear the voice of God and to obey it. We declare that we welcome God's truth and light in our churches and commit ourselves afresh to faithfully preaching the whole Word of God. We renounce all the works of Satan. Therefore, we ask You, Lord, to expose all the works of darkness that we might destroy them.

PRAYERS OF REPENTANCE FOR PASTORS AND CHURCH LEADERS
It is important that we confess our own sins before forgiving others for their sins, especially any personal or family sins of anti-Semitism. Lord, we confess that we have sinned against You in thought, word and deed. We confess and repent of our sins (only pray out what is appropriate to the individual present) of anti-Semitism, pride, self-interest, bitterness, jealousy, resentment and unforgiveness). We ask that You

would forgive us and deliver our churches and their members from any consequences of our sins. (Confess the following sins only when they are applicable.) We confess that we have not strengthened the weak, or healed the sick, or bound up the injured. We have not brought back the strays or searched for the lost. We have ruled them harshly. Please forgive us, cleanse us from all our sin, and grant that from this day forward we may express Your heart of love for Your people, and lead them gently in the ways of truth and righteousness.

PRAYER TO FORGIVE THE SINS OF OUR ANCESTORS

Lord Jesus, I unreservedly forgive my forebears, including all previous church leaders, for all the sins that they have committed which have affected us and the churches that we lead. We specifically renounce the consequences of their sins of anti-Semitism and the torture and murder of Jewish people as well as all idolatry, immorality, oppression through Communism, and all rebellion against the living God and His Son, in Jesus' name.

Heavenly Father, as children of God we declare that the power of the blood of Jesus has set us and the churches that we lead free from all the sins of our forebears. We ask that You would now free us and the churches that we lead from the consequences of all bloodguilt, as well as all occult activity in either our father or our mother's family lines (name any known occultism specifically) or in the life of our churches, and from all curses and pronouncements that have had any effect on our lives and the churches that we lead. We also ask You to set us free from all curses of sickness in the form of hereditary diseases, and from the effects of any of our forebears' sins which have affected us and our churches, in the name of Jesus, who bore the curse of sin for us that we might receive the promise of the Spirit through faith.

We repent of any personal sin of anti-Semitism and seek Your forgiveness, and we now renounce the sin of cursing the Jewish people and ask You in Your grace and mercy on the grounds of the cross of Jesus that You would release us, and the churches that we lead, and the land in which we live and worship from the curse of anti-Semitism. Amen.

CONFESSION OF SINS AGAINST OUR JEWISH BRETHREN
Dear Jewish friends, we Christians acknowledge that we and our ancestors have sinned against you and your ancestors through the sins of anti-Semitism, leading to their torture and murder. We abhor these wicked acts. We confess to you that we have not helped and protected our Jewish friends as we should have done. Please forgive us and our ancestors for these terrible sins against you, the sons of Jacob, and against the God of Abraham, Isaac and Jacob. We declare that you are a blessed people and a blessed nation and we bless you in the name of the Lord.

DECLARATION OF COMMITMENT TO THE LIVING GOD FOR HIS JEWISH PEOPLE AND THE NATION OF ISRAEL
From this day forward we shall, with God's help, be faithful to the Lord our God and His covenants, and we will defend and protect all Jewish people against all forms of anti-Semitism. We promise to pray for the peace of Jerusalem and to teach our congregations the whole counsel of God as found in the Bible, including His future will and purposes for the nation of Israel.

**GENERAL FORGIVENESS PRAYER FOR THOSE WHO HAVE CURSED
THE CHURCH AND ITS PEOPLE**
Once there is a confirmation by at least two mature believers
known for their spiritual discernment that the Lord has lifted
His curse, those praying can take authority over the presence
of any unclean spirits that have gained access to the ground.
The influence of the ruling powers over the Church and in
the town/city will be weakened by this prayer action. They
can be rendered ineffective as the local fellowships take their
stand together in unity and agreement on the Word of God
over all the power of the enemy:

We forgive every person who has directly or indirectly
cursed our churches through their words or their actions.
We include former members of our churches. We break the
power of every curse that Satan has put upon our churches.
We specifically break the power of (here you may need to
mention sickness, marital breakdown or something else that
you know Satan has afflicted the church with) every curse
affecting this church and we command every evil spirit
affecting it to go in the mighty name of Jesus Christ of
Nazareth. We ask You, Lord, to destroy every weapon that
the enemy has forged against us.

PRAYER FOR RELEASE FROM SATANIC AND WITCHCRAFT CURSES
Father, we come in the name of Jesus Christ of Nazareth,
asking that You would release us from every demon that
has been assigned to our churches through any satanic or
witchcraft ritual. We forgive all those who are opposed to
the kingdom of God and we release them into the freedom
of our forgiveness. We now break every spirit of curse over
every church represented here today and ask that You would

send Your angels to destroy any picture or any personal belonging that has been used in specific satanic or witchcraft rituals (Follow this by taking authority over evil spirits and commanding them in the Name of Jesus Christ to depart. The LORD will bring specific spirits to your mind).

CLEANSING THE GROUND FROM GOD'S CURSE FOLLOWING THE MURDER OF JEWS

The following prayer is for praying at sites where it is known that Jewish people have been murdered in cold blood.

We approach your heavenly throne LORD in the Name of Yeshua HaMaschiach (Lord Jesus Messiah), and on the ground of His shed blood. We declare that on this site here in…………………..in the year………………..a grievous crime was committed against Your ancient covenant people (state specifically what happened). Not only was this a sin against the Jews, but it was a sin against your holiness and against the covenants that you made with Noah and Abraham. We agree with your verdict on this sin. We forgive everyone involved in the murder of Your Jewish people in this place (it is appropriate to specifically mention by name, if known, those who committed such an evil crime). LORD you are just and righteous and have declared YOUR curse upon all those guilty of cursing Abraham's descendants, the nation of Israel.

It is helpful to follow this prayer by a time of silence during which the people present can pray quietly. Now the leader needs to pray, asking God to lift His curse:

Heavenly Father, You have heard our prayers of confession, renunciation and forgiveness. We ask You on the grounds of the shed blood of Jesus, Your Son, who died for the sins of the world, that in Your grace and mercy, You would lift the curse that You have sent upon this ground and from the people of this city/town and especially from the churches in this place.

Where there has been no funeral service, it is important to commit the human spirits of those who have died, to the Lord. The basis for this comes from the words of Jesus, who before He died committed His Spirit into the hands of His Father (Luke 23:46):

Heavenly Father, we commit into Your hands the spirits of those who died here.

During the prayer action it is important to be sensitive to the voice of the Lord and to adapt all prayer according to the leading of the Holy Spirit. When there is a sense of peace that the prayer action has been completed, praying a blessing upon the local Jewish community can conclude the meeting.

BLESSING ISRAEL

The Word of God teaches us that we must love others not in word and tongue but in deed and truth (1 John 3:18). Our love for Israel and the Jewish people must have a practical outworking. It is insufficient to say that we love Jewish people if we are not seeking to befriend them. Giving money to enable the *aliyah* from our own financial resources is one very practical demonstration of love, and the apostle Paul encourages us to do this (Romans 15:26,27). The words of Jesus teach us how our love can and should be expressed:

Then the King will say to those on His right hand, 'Come, you blessed of My Father, inherit the kingdom prepared for you from the foundation of the world: for I was hungry and you gave Me food; I was thirsty and you gave Me drink; I was a stranger and you took Me in; I was naked and you clothed Me; I was sick and you visited Me; I was in prison and you came to Me.'

(MATTHEW 25:34–36)

PRAYER FOR THE *ALIYAH* HIGHWAYS

On this day, when the Lord has released us from the curse of anti-Semitism, we take authority over every demonic power that has gained access to the *aliyah* highways through our sins and the sins of our ancestors to block, hinder or prevent *aliyah* taking place from this town/city or country. In the name of Jesus we break the power of Satan and his demons and order them to release the *aliyah* highways now.

CHAPTER 5

AUTHORITY AND POWER IN INTERCESSORY PRAYER

Spiritual authority and power are essential in relation to intercessory prayer. When we proclaim God's Word and intercede on behalf of God's *aliyah* purposes for Israel, we must also know the difference between authority and power. Equally important is knowledge of the extent to which the intercessor can exercise authority and power, keeping within the Lord's protection. Intercessory prayer brings the individual into the spiritual realms where Satan and the powers of darkness resist the will of God.

A WARNING FROM SCRIPTURE

Unless we are to become casualties, we need to have a good understanding of the nature and work of demonic powers. There has been little teaching in the Church on this subject, and this has led to spiritual casualties worldwide, not least on the mission field. For example, many have been wrongly taught that because Satan has been defeated at the cross, he poses no danger to the believer. This is wrong; one only has to consider the warnings in Scripture (1 Peter 5:8,9). It is vital to understand the authority given to us as disciples of Christ, with respect to its extent and its limitations (Luke 10:19; Acts 16:7).

We must neither fail to exercise the full extent of the authority given to us by Jesus (Luke 10:18,19), nor dare to go beyond our God-given authority. For example, we can only pray effectively in accordance with the Word of God as directed by the Holy Spirit (John 15:7). This means that we must seek the Lord before any prayer action. Although every prayer action requires a leader (it is important that people are kept to the agreed agenda) and considerable preparation, it is vital that before the prayer action every participant understands the purpose of the action and is in full unity and agreement with it (Psalm 133; Acts 2:1; 4:24).

GOD IS THE SOURCE OF ALL AUTHORITY AND POWER

All authority in heaven and on earth has its source in the living God – Father, Son and Holy Spirit (Romans 13:1–5). This authority is exercised in the heavenly realms by spirit beings and upon the earth by human beings. This authority is a delegated authority: God shares His authority with humankind. Both Adam and Eve were told by God to 'subdue [the earth]; have dominion over the fish of the sea, over the birds of the air, and over every living thing …' (Genesis 1:28). Governments are given authority to govern their people, and have a responsibility to govern fairly and justly in keeping with God's holy law. Our responsibility is to pray for all those who exercise authority over us, whether secular or spiritual (2 Timothy 2:1–4; Hebrews 13:18).

GOD DELEGATES HIS AUTHORITY AND POWER

Because God's authority is delegated, everyone who exercises authority must give an account to God as to how it was exercised (Hebrews 13:17; Romans 14:12). If this authority is to achieve God's purpose, it can only be used according to God's moral and spiritual laws as expressed in the Word of God. This applies to both secular and spiritual authority. Those who disregard God's laws in the exercise of His authority will sow confusion and destruction and will bring themselves under the judgement of God.

It is important that disciples of Jesus do not to go beyond their delegated authority. In 1 Samuel 13, King Saul assumed the role of a priest, offered the burnt offering against the Law of Moses, and was rejected as king as a consequence (1 Samuel 13:13,14). He had the ability to offer the burnt offering – the power – but he did not have the authority – the right – to do it.

AUTHORITY AND POWER

The Greek word for authority is *exousia* and for power is *dunamis*. Authority is the right to exercise power. Power is the ability to exercise authority. All human authority is limited. Those in authority are also subject to a higher authority and cannot go beyond certain boundaries. Public officials cannot use their authority and power to go beyond the law, otherwise they themselves become subject to the penalty of the law. In a democratic society, no one is above the law.

THE EXAMPLE OF A LAW ENFORCEMENT OFFICER

In most Western countries, a resident of that country can make a citizen's arrest. This can only be done when someone is observed to be committing a crime. In contrast, a law enforcement officer (police officer) can arrest someone on suspicion that a crime has been committed. The difficulty in making a citizen's arrest is that although the right or authority is present, the power may not be. To reinforce authority, law enforcement officers are identified by their uniform and have a variety of restraints available to them, and in most Western nations, they carry a pistol.

THE EXAMPLE OF A BOXER

When a boxer hits his opponent in the boxing ring, he is not arrested! Even if his opponent should die as a consequence of a blow, he has not broken the law. If, however, he hits someone outside the boxing ring, he has broken the law. The difference between the two situations is the following: in the boxing ring, he had two necessary components: authority to hit his opponent and the power to do so. If he hits someone outside the boxing ring, there is one component missing: authority. The extent or the limit of his authority lies within the confines of the boxing ring.

PRAYER INTERCESSORS

Intercession requires both authority and power. Both are delegated, given by the One who has authority and power, the Lord Jesus Christ (Matthew 28:18–20). Jesus has been given all authority in heaven and on earth (Matthew 28:18) and He has delegated His authority and power to His disciples (Luke 10:18,19; John 14:12).

RELATIONSHIP TO THE SOURCE OF AUTHORITY

The key to using this authority and power is relationship and fellowship with Jesus. When those exercising authority are not themselves living in obedience to the source of authority, what they end up relying on is their position, but in fact they are merely exercising soul power or human willpower. This will impact the other's soul and lead to conflict. All those who exercise authority must themselves be willing to submit to authority as exercised by leaders put in place by God (Hebrews 13:17).

Real authority proceeds from the spirit of the one exercising authority and impacts the spirit of the person on whom it is exercised. The Holy Spirit is vital in the process of hearing the voice of God.

The ability of an intercessor to hear the voice of God is essential; it is directly linked to the issue of personal wholeness. Many believers are unaware that they need healing and deliverance arising from the consequences of the past. Prayer warriors must be able to discern and reject all deceiving spirits who masquerade as the genuine voice of the Holy Spirit.

> For if he who comes preaches another Jesus whom we have not preached, or if you receive a different spirit which you have not received, or a different gospel which you have not accepted – you may well put up with it!
>
> (2 CORINTHIANS 11:4)

It is important to take the warnings concerning the last days of this present age given by Jesus. 'Take heed that no one deceives you. For many will come in My name ...' (Matthew 24:4,5). In a similar vein, the apostle Paul warns Timothy that in the latter times he should be aware that some will be taken in by deceiving spirits (1 Timothy 4:1–5).

DIFFERENT KINDS OF AUTHORITY

The following teaching is based upon Tom Marshall's teaching in his book, *Understanding Leadership*, identifies different Greek words for the English word 'authority', each used in a specific context or activity.[95]

TASK AUTHORITY

He explains that task authority is the most direct form of authority. The leader gives instructions, and the participants must understand the instructions and carry them out. This kind of authority is used also for simple tasks such as moving an object like a crate or a piano. Unless the order to lift is not restricted to one person, confusion reigns and physical harm can be the result. This is the kind of authority that works in the military or in dangerous situations or emergencies. This authority is an essential element in concerted prayer action such as a prayer journey. It requires a lot of trust. Task authority also works with small children to establish their obedience before they can understand.

TEACHING AUTHORITY

The aim of teaching authority is that someone learns how to do something. This process involves simplification, explanation and illustration. It involves understanding principles and is therefore open to question. It is important that disciples of Jesus act like the Bereans and check the Bible to see if what is taught can be verified and is in line with Scripture (Acts 17:10,11).

SPIRITUAL AUTHORITY

Authority in the spiritual and moral realms is to help people change character – to be rather than to do. They must be free, therefore, to make a personal decision. This is a moral choice; people can only agree on the basis of their conscience. Unless individuals are free to make their own decision on the basis of their conscience, any change that occurs will be a mere outward change that does not come from a willing heart. In non-moral matters there is a requirement that respect for differences of opinion is recognised, because people are different. Cults go for conformity and total agreement by all. However, some matters are clearly defined in Scripture, and rejection of true spiritual authority will always negatively affect the one who rejected it. God recognises the individual's personal choice, even when it shuts Him out (Revelation 3:20). Spiritual authority includes binding and loosing. Binding is the act of restraining or restricting on earth those things that are being retrained or restricted in heaven. Loosing is the act of setting free on earth those things being freed in heaven (Matthew 18:18,19). We are to bind what God binds and loose what Satan binds, to loose what God looses and bind what Satan looses.

RULING SPIRITS

The call of an intercessor brings the individual into conflict with the powers of darkness. This is true for all those who seek to live a godly life in Christ Jesus and whose aim is to obey Him (2 Timothy 3:12; Revelation 12:17). The book of Ephesians teaches us that '... we do not wrestle against flesh and blood, but against principalities, against powers, against the rulers of the darkness of this age, against spiritual hosts of wickedness in the heavenly places' (Ephesians 6:12). Ruling spirits act on behalf of Satan to carry out his will in opposing those who are involved in the proclamation and establishment of the kingdom of God. Angels act on behalf of God and His people to bless God's people and to overcome the activity of evil spirits. They serve those who belong to the Lord (Hebrews 1:14). We see a glimpse of their activity in the book of Daniel. Chapter 10 records that on one occasion Daniel sought God in prayer (Daniel 9:3) following his reading of the prophet Jeremiah. He realised that the time of the Babylonian captivity was coming to an end, and he felt prompted to seek God for the fulfilment of His Word.

THE PRINCE OF THE KINGDOM OF PERSIA

Daniel's prayer was immediately heard in heaven, but it was three weeks before Daniel was given the understanding he sought. His answer was brought by an angelic visitor, probably the angel Gabriel (Daniel 8:16,17). The angel informed Daniel that he had been sent, it would appear, almost immediately, but that it had taken him twenty-one days to get to Daniel because he had met resistance in the heavenly realms (Daniel 10:10–14). The implication is that he had been attacked by the demonic prince of Persia and had to call on angelic help. He called on the archangel Michael, described as 'one of the chief princes' (Daniel 10:13) of the angelic hosts.

We learn at least three things from this account. First, that God hears prayer that is according to His will and based upon His Word. Secondly, He always sends an answer, although it may not result in an angelic visitation. Thirdly, we may have to wait for the answer because there is a spiritual battle occurring between angels and demons in the heavenly realms, or because it is not yet His timing.

Clearly, the demonic princes mentioned in the book of Daniel are as active today as they were in ancient times. We looked at the authority and power of Satan in *Reclaiming the Ground* chapter 1, pp. 16,17). For example, what spirit do you think is behind the nation of Iran, modern-day Persia? Could this demonic prince of Persia be the spirit behind Islam? For it was in Iran in 1979, during the revolution, that Ayatollah Khomeini declared the assumption of Allah's rule. Since that time Iranian-sponsored terrorism has increased worldwide. Iran seems to ignore the rule of law adhered to by civilised nations and is intent on developing its own nuclear programme. Why does Iran persist with the development of a nuclear capability in the face of such severe international sanctions?

When we read statements made by Iranian leaders, we may be forgiven for thinking that the purpose is to use a nuclear bomb against Israel. When Mahmoud Ahmadinejad was President of Iran, he told an annual anti-Israel protest in Tehran on Friday, 17 August 2012, that the Jewish state was a 'cancerous tumor' that would soon be excised.

> The Zionist regime and the Zionists are a cancerous tumor. The nations of the region will soon finish off the usurper Zionists in the Palestinian land ... A new Middle East will definitely be formed. With the grace of God and help of the nations, in the new Middle East there will be no trace of the Americans and Zionists.[96]

The words 'cancerous tumor' echo those of Adolf Hitler. When these words were spoken in the 1930s, the nations of the world stood by and did practically nothing to help the Jewish people. Yes, there were brave individuals who risked their lives to help Jews. I wonder, are we going to see a repeat of history?

AUTHORITY OVER RULING SPIRITS

It is vital that we understand the nature and extent of our spiritual authority. The Lord Jesus told His disciples, 'Behold, I give you the authority to trample on serpents and scorpions, and over all the power of the enemy, and nothing shall by any means hurt you' (Luke 10:19). We may find ourselves in spiritual battles wrestling with ruling spirits, but they cannot resist the will of God as we stand upon the Word of God. We can't destroy Satan and his demons, only resist and destroy their works (1 John 3:8b). This does not mean that we can do anything we like, but only that which the Holy Spirit leads us to do. For example, we cannot cast out the ruling spirits that inhabit the heavenly realms as we can the demons that inhabit humankind. However, I do believe that we can and must render their influence null and void over our cities and churches as we stand in agreement together on the Word of God.

SPIRITUAL WARFARE

If we fail to take the battle to the enemy, it will not stop him from attacking us. In any war, defence alone is insufficient; the enemy must be attacked and destroyed. Some years ago, I learned something about military strategy as expressed through the principles of warfare. They apply also to spiritual warfare:

- Selection and maintenance of the aim;
- Maintenance of momentum;
- Offensive action;
- Administration;
- Concentration of force or economy of effort;
- Surprise;
- Security – including intelligence: know your enemy.

SPIRITUAL PROTECTION

In any battle there are casualties. To ensure that we do not become a casualty we need to take heed of the warnings in Scripture (1 Peter 5:8). Ephesians chapter 6 provides understanding of how we may protect our spirit as we engage in spiritual warfare. Those called to intercessory prayer for the *aliyah* are praying according to God's prophetic word for the opening of the *aliyah* highways and the removal of the blockages in the spiritual realm (Isaiah 62:10). As Satan seeks to oppose and hinder the will of God, this means destroying the works of the enemy (1 John 3:8b).

In spiritual warfare, we enforce the will of God; both His general will and His specific will. The source of our authority is His authority that He has delegated to us (Luke 10:19). The grounds for our authority is the victory of Jesus Christ over sin, Satan and all his works through His death and resurrection and His current reign at the right hand of the Father in heaven (2 Corinthians 10:4; 6:7; Romans 13:12; Ephesians 6:10–18). One of the weapons of our warfare is the Word of God and its proclamation, which is powerful and effective (Hebrews 4:12). A single vision and purpose is vital for any prayer action (Proverbs 29:18). Jesus taught that a house divided against itself cannot stand (Luke 11:17). The following are the necessary conditions and activities, for the exercise of spiritual authority and power:

- Christian discipleship demands a willingness to lay down our own life and our will in order to seek God's will. The Christian disciple must learn to abstain from sinful actions and follow Him (Luke 9:23; 1 Peter 2:11);
- It is only through our relationship with Jesus and the maintenance of intimate and regular fellowship with Him that the believer can experience the victory of the cross: '... without Me you can do nothing' (John 15:4,5);
- Living in the power of the Holy Spirit (Galatians 5:16; Ephesians 5:18);
- Living in unity with one another: if we do not stand together in unity of fellowship and purpose, we will fall (Psalm 133);
- Understanding our authority and power (Luke 10:17–19);
- Praying and interceding in the power of the Holy Spirit (Ephesians 6:18);
- Preaching and teaching in the power of the Holy Spirit (1 Corinthians 2:4);
- Destroying the works of Satan and overcoming evil by doing good (Romans 12:21).

Edmund Burke once remarked, 'It is necessary only for the good man to do nothing for evil to triumph.'[97] We usually do nothing and expect God to do all the fighting for us. We need to ditch our defensive attitude and adopt an offensive one, for we need to lay hold of the sword of the Spirit of God. We are called to be warriors as well as worshippers.

THE SPIRITUAL ARMOUR
EPHESIANS 6:10–20

- We must 'be strong in the Lord and in the power of His might'. This strength and power comes from our union with Jesus (v. 10).

- If we are to stand against the devil's schemes, then we must 'Put on the whole armor of God' (v. 11).

- Our struggle is not against flesh and blood, but 'against principalities, against powers, against the rulers of the darkness of this age' and the 'hosts of wickedness in the heavenly places' (v. 12).

- We are admonished for the second time to put on the 'whole armor of God' and when we have done everything, to stand. We need to stand firm; in other words, we need to hold our ground (v. 13).

- We must stand firm with the belt of truth buckled around our waist (v. 14). The belt of truth will protect us in the measure that we ourselves walk in the truth. It is not automatic.

- It is also necessary for us to put on the 'breastplate of righteousness' (v. 14; 1 Thessalonians 5:8; Romans 13:8). Godly living is essential to effective life and service.

- 'and having shod your feet with the preparation of the gospel of peace' – soldiers must wear their shoes at all times when on active duty (v. 15). It means RFA – ready for action, ready for anything. When on active duty, military personnel never take their boots off.

- In addition to all this, we must take up the 'shield of faith' with which to extinguish the 'fiery darts' of the evil one (v. 16). This means that we must be active and not passive as we follow Jesus.

- '... take the helmet of salvation' (v. 17). Protection of the head in any battle is essential. It will guard the thought life and protect us from the father of lies.
- Take 'the sword of the Spirit, which is the word of God' (v. 17). A deep knowledge of the Word of God is essential; there is no substitute for this.
- We must also pray in the Spirit with all kinds of prayer on all occasions (v. 18).
- To be constantly filled with the Holy Spirit is a command (Ephesians 5:18).
- BE ALERT ALWAYS (1 Thessalonians 5:8). It's no good being fully trained and equipped if we are asleep on duty!

IN CONCLUSION

The Church has lost its connection with its Jewish foundation. Consequently, it cannot make full sense of the Bible. The early disciples were Jewish. There were no Gentiles present on the day of Pentecost – although there may have been proselytes – when the Holy Spirit fell upon those believers. Gentiles are not mentioned until we get to Acts chapters 8 and 10. It is we Gentiles who were once strangers to the covenants that now through faith in Messiah Jesus have been joined to the commonwealth of Israel.

> that at that time you were without Christ, being aliens from the commonwealth of Israel and strangers from the covenants of promise, having no hope and without God in the world. But now in Christ Jesus you who once were far off have been brought near by the blood of Christ.
>
> (EPHESIANS 2:12,13)

In other words, it is us that have joined the believing remnant, and not the other way round. The early Church had authority to heal the sick. In comparison, the Church of the twenty-first century has little authority. Having been involved in healing and deliverance for many years, I have to admit that we do not have the authority that the early Church had. For example, we see little physical healing. It is fair to say that healing ministries have seen more healing than the local church has, but even allowing for this, their success is limited. Sadly, healing is often not present at all in many churches.

This gap between the experience of the early disciples as demonstrated in the New Testament and present-day experience has puzzled me for years. I sensed in my spirit that it was not the unwillingness of God to pour out His Spirit in power upon the Church, but that sin was present somewhere. I began to think of possible sins that would have the effect of limiting the power of the Holy Spirit. There is no doubt a lack of Christian discipleship today. However, following the revelation that God has graciously given me concerning Israel, I believe that the problem is much deeper than that, and it affects the corporate anointing upon the whole body of Christ. I am now able to identify at least two unresolved issues that grieve the Holy Spirit. These are grievous sins in the sight of God concerning which the Church must repent of otherwise the Church will continue to be weak and lacking authority. The first one is the disconnection from our Jewish roots. The second is the sin of anti-Semitism. I recently read something written by a German pastor from Tübingen that to me has a distinct ring of truth:

To this day, silence and indifference toward injustice against Israel and the Jewish people are the outward signs of a deeply-hidden anti-Semitism that Christianity has carried in its very heart ever since it separated from its Jewish roots. By now the Hellenistic spirit has penetrated deeply into many churches and congregations in the form of postmodern secular humanism. *If they want to regain their original authority, they first have to find their way back to their Hebrew roots.*[98]

The time is short and we are getting nearer and nearer to the second coming of the Son of God. The time for the judgement of the world is drawing upon us.

Therefore let us not sleep, as others do, but let us watch and be sober. For those who sleep, sleep at night, and those who get drunk are drunk at night. But let us who are of the day be sober, putting on the breastplate of faith and love, and as a helmet the hope of salvation.

(1 THESSALONIANS 5:6–8)

ENDNOTES

PREFACE

[1] *Israel 101*, English pdf, p. 12.
[2] http://news.bbc.co.uk/1/hi/world/middle_east/4912198.stm (accessed 29/08/2013).

INTRODUCTION

[3] Ken Hepworth, *Reclaiming the Ground: The Biblical Basis and Practice of Breaking Curses on Land and Cleansing Buildings from Evil Spirits* (Lancaster: Sovereign World, 2003, 2008).
[4] Matthew 1:2; 8:11; 22:32; Acts 3:13; 7:8,32.
[5] Steve Malz, *Outcast Nation-Israel, The Jews… and You* (UK: Saffron Planet, www.sppublishing.com, 2012,).
[6] 'When the plain sense of Scripture makes common sense, seek no other sense; therefore, take every word at its primary, ordinary, usual, literal meaning unless the facts of the immediate context, studied in light of related passages and axiomatic and fundamental truths, indicate clearly otherwise.' http://www.spiritandtruth.org/teaching/documents/articles/25/25.htm?x=x (accessed 19/08/2014).
[7] NKJV Study Bible, copyright 1982 by Thomas Nelson Inc., p. xv.

CHAPTER 1

8 http://www.ngomonitor.org/editions/v4n03/
AJIRI3UNInhospitable101705.pdf> (accessed 19/08/2013).

9 http://honestreporting.com/israel-daily-news-stream-08182013/
(accessed 19/08/2013).

10 http://www.bbc.co.uk/news/world-middle-east-13481924 > (accessed
16/07/2103).

11 http://www.haaretz.com/news/haaretz-exclusive-eu-draft-document-on-
division-of-jerusalem-1.3029 > (accessed 16/07/2013).

12 https://www.thecst.org.uk/docs/Incidents%20Report%202012.pdf.
(accessed 15/07/2013).

13 http://humanities.tau.ac.il/roth/2012-09-10-07-07-36/antisemitism
(accessed 15/07/2013).

14 http://www.jewishvirtuallibrary.org/jsource/biography/WilhelmMarr.
html (accessed 15/07/2013).

15 http://www.palestinecampaign.org/about/ (accessed 23/08/2014).

16 http://www.bdsmovement.net (accessed 19/08/2013).

17 *The Daily Telegraph*, 28 August 2103, p. 14.

18 http://www.bdsmovement.net/activecamps/divestment
(accessed 23/08/2013).

19 http://www.bdsmovement.net/activecamps/sanctions
(accessed 23/08/2013).

20 Colonel Richard Kemp was the guest speaker at a Zionist Federation
Gala Dinner in London at which the author was present.

21 http://eipa.eu.com/category/information-centre/arabs-israel/arab-
recognition-of-jewish-state/ [accessed 08/10/2013].

22 http://www.jewishvirtuallibrary.org/jsource/Peace/cd2000art.html
(accessed 03/09/2013).

23 *Israel 101* English pdf, p. 11.

24 http://www.unrwa.org/etemplate.php?id=86
(accessed 26/08/2013).

25 *Israel 101*, English pdf.

26 Ibid.

27 Ibid.

28 http://electronicintifada.net/content/uk-rewrites-war-crimes-law-israels-
request/10446 (accessed 15/07/2012).

29 http://www.jpost.com/Middle-East/Abbas-wants-not-a-single-Israeli-in-
future-Palestinian-state-321470 (accessed 20/08/2013).

30 *Gustav Scheller, Operation Exodus: Prophecy Being Fulfilled,*

20th Anniversary Edition (Bournemouth: Ebenezer Emergency Fund International, 2011).

[31] http://www.jewishvirtuallibrary.org/jsource/biography/ben_yehuda. html [.accessed 07/10/2013].

[32] Ibid.

[33] My term of office came to an end on 31 March 2013.

[34] *Malcolm Hedding, 'The Folly of Fulfillment Theology' (2012) <http://int.icej.org/news/commentary/folly-fulfillment-theology>*[accessed 07/10/2013}. N.B Type into the ICEJ web-site Replacement Theology]

[35] *Ignatius, Bishop of Antioch martyred* AD *117: 'If anyone celebrates the Passover along with the Jews, or receives the emblems of their feasts, he is a partaker with those who killed the Lord and His Apostles':* Fred Wright, *Words from the Scroll of Fire* (Jerusalem, Israel: Four Corners Publishing, 1994), p. 92.

[36] Colin Chapman, *Whose Promised Land?* (Oxford: Lion, 1983, 1992, 2002).

[37] Stephen Sizer, *Christian Zionism: Road-map to Armageddon?* (London: Inter-Varsity Press, 2004).

[38] http://stephensizer.blogspot.co.uk/2008/11/revd-dr-john-stott-on-christian-zionism.html (accessed 15/07/2013).

[39] Barry E. Horner, *Future Israel: Why Christian Anti-Judaism Must be Challenged* (Nashville, Tennessee: B & H Academic), ISBN 13:978-0-8054-4627-2.

[40] Boris Zabarko, *Holocaust in the Ukraine* (Middlesex: Valentine Mitchel & Co. Ltd., 2005).

CHAPTER 2

[41] http://www.science.co.il/Arab-Israeli-conflict.asp (accessed 26/08/2013).

[42] 'The recent Palestinian Authority report stating that the Western Wall has no religious or historical significance to the Jewish people is sadly yet another attempt at political historical revisionism ...' http://www.jpost. com/Opinion/OpEdContributors/Article.aspx?id=19698 (accessed 11 August 2012).

[43] http://zionistfederation.blogspot.co.uk/2012/02/zionist-federation-lobby-day-great_16.html (accessed 15/07/2013).

[44] http://www.britannica.com/EBchecked/topic/521598/Conference-of-San-Remo (accessed 15/07/2013).

[45] http://www2.ohchr.org/english/bodies/hrcouncil/specialsession/9/FactFindingMission.htm (accessed 15/07/2013).

[46] http://www.washingtonpost.com/opinions/reconsidering-the-goldstone-report-on-israel-and-war crimes/2011/04/01/AFg111JC_story.html (accessed 15/07/2013).

[47] http://www.ynetnews.com/articles/0,7340,L-3888870,00.html (accessed 15/07/2013).

[48] http://www.cbsnews.com/2100-215_162-655409.html (accessed 15/07/2013).

[49] http://www.historyofwar.org/articles/concepts_hijacking.html (accessed 15/07/2013).

[50] http://news.bbc.co.uk/1/hi/uk_politics/8219864.stm (accessed 15/07/2013).

[51] http://www.standwithus.com/booklets/IL101/, p. 22 (accessed 15/07/2013).

[52] http://mideastweb.org/hamas.htm (accessed 15/07/2013).

[53] Ibid.

[54] http://www.bbc.co.uk/religion/religions/islam/beliefs/jihad_1.shtml (accessed 19/08/2013).

[55] Fars News Agency, Iran. Published: 16 August 2012.

[56] Sam Solomon and E. Al Maqdisi, Al-Yahud, *The Islamic Doctrine of Enmity & the Jews* (Pilcrow Press.com, 2010), pp. 154–164.

[57] Qur'an, 37:102.

[58] See the video on *The Education of Arab Palestinian Children* at the following web address: http://www.science.co.il/Arab-Israeli-conflict.asp (accessed 26/08/2013).

[59] http://elderofziyon.blogspot.co.uk/2005/03/ideal-palestinian-woman.html#.UjiO1RZRaMN (accessed 17/09/2013).

[60] http://www.jewishvirtuallibrary.org/jsource/arabs/patext2006.html (accessed 23/08/2013).

[61] David Rausch, *Legacy of Hatred: Why Christians Must Not Forget the Holocaust* Baker Pub. Group, 1990 (ISBN 0801077583), p. 27. http://www.historyworld.net/wrldhis/PlainTextHistories.asp?historyid=ab54 (accessed 15/07/2013).

[62] Martin Luther, *On the Jews and Their Lies* http://www.preteristarchive.com/Books/1543_luther_jews.html (accessed 30 April 2012).

[63] <http://christiandiscussionsmsn.yuku.com/topic/8766#.UlLX_BZqeMM> [accessed 07/10/2013].

[64] Fred Wright, *Words From the Scroll of Fire* (Jerusalem, Israel: Four Corners Publishing, 1994), p. 92.

[65] Ibid, p. 102.

[66] Ibid, p. 105.

CHAPTER 3

[67] http://mfa.gov.il/MFA/AboutIsrael/Pages/default.aspx [accessed 07/10/2013].

[68] *Israel 101*, 'Stand With Us'. <http://www.standwithus.com/ONLINE_ BOOKLETS/Israel%20101%20English, p.40> [accessed -7/10/2013].

[69] *Israel 101*, *'Stand With Us'*. http://www.standwithus.com/*ONLINE_ BOOKLETS*/Israel%20101%20English/ (accessed 29 September 2012).

[70] Fred Wright, *Father, Forgive Us* (London: Monarch Books, 2002), p. 33.

[71] Dina Porat and Ken Stern, 'Defining Anti-Semitism', *research article*, (Lester and Sally Entin Faculty of Humanities, Stephen Roth Institute for the Study of Anti-Semitism and Racism, The Kantor Center for the Study of Contemporary European Jewry, 2003-4), http://www.tau.ac.il/Anti-Semitism/asw2003-4/porat.htm (accessed 29 September 2012). Used with permission.

[72] Dina Porat and Ken Stern, *'Defining Anti-Semitism'* (accessed 29 September 2012). Used with permission.

[73] Ibid.

[74] Willem J. Glashouwer, *Why Israel?* (Pescara- Italy: Destiny Image Europe, 2007), p. 119.

[75] Peter Horrobin, *Healing Through Deliverance: The Foundation and Practice of Deliverance Ministry* (UK: Sovereign World, 1991, 2003, 2008).

[76] http://www.bdsmovement.net (accessed 15/07/2013).

[77] Israel 101 *Israel, English.pdf*, p. 16

[78] <http://www.jpost.com/Middle-East/Abbas-at-the-UNGA-Israeli-Palestinian-peace-means-Arab-recognition-of-Israel-327186 [.accessed 07/10/2013].

[79] http://www.usasurvival.org/ck2.07-2.11.html (accessed 16/07/2013).

[80] Bat Ye'or, *Eurabia: The Euro-Arab Axis (Cranbury, NJ, USA: Associated University Press, 2005).*

[81] http://www.bbc.co.uk/news/uk-16522447 (accessed 16/07/2013).

[82] http://www.ec4i.org/images/stories/Jerusalem_Issue_brief_21_ Dec_2010.pdf (accessed 16/07/2013).

[83] http://www.ushmm.org/wlc/en/article.php?ModuleId=10007392 [accessed 08/10/2013].

[84] http://www.cbn.com/cbnnews/insideisrael/2013/July/Islamist-Assault-Saturday-Kill-Jews-Sunday-Kill-Christans/ [accessed 08/10/2013].

[85] http://www.bbc.co.uk/news/world-africa-24191606

[86] http://www.bbc.co.uk/news/world-africa-24283901. [accessed 08/10/2013]. <http://www.spectator.co.uk/features/9034771/surviving-nairobis-westgate-mall-siege/ [accessed 08/10/2013

CHAPTER 4

[87] http://www.bl.uk/learning/timeline/item103483.html (accessed 16/07/2013).

[88] http://www.yorkcastle.com/pages/jewish_history.html (accessed 16/07/2013).

[89] http://www.bbc.co.uk/religion/religions/judaism/history/350.shtml (accessed 16/07/2013).

[90] http://www.jewishvirtuallibrary.org/jsource/Judaism/expulsion.html (accessed 16/07/2013).

[91] http://www.guardian.co.uk/commentisfree/2011/mar/16/germany-overcoming-past-arab-dictatorships (accessed 16/07/2013).

[92] http://www.iearn.org/hgp/aeti/aeti-1998-no-frames/holocaust-ed-in-germany.htm (accessed 16/07/2013).

[93] http://paganwiccan.about.com/b/2013/06/22/english-witchcraft-laws-repealed-6221951.htm (accessed 16/07/2013).

[94] http://www.jonasclark.com/spiritual-warfare-prayer/when-christian-witches-attack-you.html (accessed 17/09/2013).

CHAPTER 5

[95] Tom Marshall, *Understanding Leadership* (Lancaster: Sovereign World, 1991), pp. 100-113 (Tom Marshall gave me permission to use his material in my teaching. I have not quoted directly).

[96] President Mahmoud Ahmadinejad – Quds Day Address, 17 August 2012; AFP.com, published 17 August 2012.

[97] Edmund Burke, *The Oxford Dictionary of Quotations, new edition* (Oxford: OUP, 1994, 2001), p. 148.

[98] Jobst Bittner, *Breaking the Veil of Silence* (Tübingen: TOS Publishing, 2013), p. 178 (my italics).

ABOUT THE
AUTHOR

Ken Hepworth has served the local Church for over forty years as evangelist, pastor and teacher. He is a man with a heart for God's people – both the body of Christ and the Jewish nation. He has a desire to see the Church, locally and globally, become all it is destined to be in Christ. This passion has placed him at the cutting edge of healing and deliverance issues, having served for many years with Ellel Ministries as a Bible teacher and prayer counsellor. Ken's experience with Ellel Ministries led him to write what still remains as one of the most informative books available on spiritual warfare, *Reclaiming the Ground*, published by Sovereign World Ltd.

Through his reading of the Bible, Ken has understood the importance of the Jewish people in the will and purposes of God, and is convinced that God has not forsaken or abandoned His first Covenant people. He has a passion to expose anti-Semitism and to dispel false teachings such as

Replacement Theology. He holds a BA (Hons) in German Studies from Lancaster University.

For the last five years he's had the privilege of being the UK Chairman of Ebenezer Operation Exodus. Through this work, Ken was able to research and pray into the worldwide foundations and influences of anti-Semitism. His work is presently dedicated to the ongoing restoration of Israel in accordance with Biblical prophecy, providing practical guidance for those called to be intercessors for Israel on how to cleanse land and lives from the consequences of Jewish blood shedding. Ken has been happily married to Jean since 1965. They have three sons and five grandchildren.

You may contact Ken on kenhepworth@icloud.com

Lightning Source UK Ltd.
Milton Keynes UK
UKOW06f1646130416

272177UK00001B/2/P